IT'S NEVER TOO LATE
TO HAVE A HAPPY CHILDHOOD

FROM ADVERSITY TO RESILIENCE

Ben Furman

BT Press

IT'S NEVER TOO LATE
TO HAVE A HAPPY CHILDHOOD
FROM ADVERSITY TO RESILIENCE

Ben Furman

BT Press

Originally published and printed by Werner Söderström Oy - Finland,
Juva 1997

English edition first published October 1998
Published by BT Press
17 Avenue Mansions, Finchley Road, London NW3 7AX

© Ben Furman 1997
Introduction © Chris Iveson 1998

Designed by Alex Gollner

No part of this publication may be reproduced, stored in a retrieval
system, or transmitted in any form or by any means, electronic,
mechanical, photocopying, recording or otherwise, without the prior
permission of the copyright owner.

ISBN 1 871697 72 7

CONTENTS

Dedications

This book is dedicated to my parents for all they have given me.

I thank my mother for teaching me a sense of proportion and an ability to look at what is good in people rather than what is bad.

I thank my father for giving me something that he learned from *his* father: incurable optimism and a sense of humour, an ability to find something amusing even in serious situations.

ACKNOWLEDGEMENTS

I haven't written this book alone. I have come across a wealth of scientific and not so scientific literature on the subject and have realised how topical the issue of surviving a difficult childhood is. The subject seems to interest so many experts that one can speak fairly of a new trend in psychology.

I have discussed the significance of childhood experiences with many people and also initiated Internet discussions on both domestic and international forums. These conversations have played an important role in the formation of this book. They have not only encouraged me to pursue the issue but have also provided me with a wealth of useful ideas.

I am especially thankful to those numerous people who, through their personal contributions, have participated in writing this book. In the autumn of 1996, two Finnish magazines published a sample of my interviews and a note that I was writing a book on the subject. In that note I asked readers who had had difficult childhoods to write to me about their experiences, answering three main questions:

1. What do you think helped you survive your difficult child-hood?
2. What have you learned from your difficult childhood?
3. In what way have you managed to have later on in your life the kind of experiences that you were deprived of as a child?

I received some 300 touching replies, and I do not exagger-ate when I say that these letters really opened my eyes. I thought I was able to explain theoretically how even a difficult childhood may later on in life begin to seem valuable. But after reading that mountain of letters I became convinced that a human being appears to be a creature capable of surviving almost anything. I arrived at the belief that people can regard their past – including even the most excessive sufferings – as a source of strength rather than of weakness.

Many of the people who wrote to me offered their support to my project and said that they were pleased to know that there was someone out there willing to question the simplistic belief in the inevitably fateful significance of a difficult childhood.

As one correspondent wrote: "Often I see red when someone mindlessly labels a teenager or an adult as destined to have a certain kind of a future just because of his or her childhood. Personally I think that a 'difficult childhood' does not inevitably lead to an unhappier adulthood than growing up in a so-called normal family."

"In spite of it all, I'm really glad that I've managed to just push on even though life is hard for me. I'm not a drunk or a loser. I have kids and a job. Many people wonder why my brother and I didn't become drunks although Mum and Dad did. What would they know? They are always ready to label kids whose parents are alcoholics as no-good losers. I hope that your book will emphasise the good and the positive, that life is worth living even though your childhood was not happy."

"Even though your childhood was difficult, you really can have it either good or bad when you're an adult. People often say, 'like father, like son'; that you're a product of your upbringing, that you can't grow up a sound person if your basic feeling of security has been lost as a child. There are plenty of real-life examples of people who've made it as adults despite their childhood experiences. You grow as a person through various life experiences and I've been given a chance to grow up a lot. My childhood has definitely left a scar on my soul but I still enjoy my life and know I can tackle life's challenges. It's good that someone is challenging the myths of childhood because a lot of people think that way."

I was especially delighted to find that many of the people who wrote to me explained that writing about their experiences had turned out to be a helpful experience in itself. Some examples:

"I felt relieved, a bit more balanced and better when I got to write about these things. Writing is for me a therapeutic activity; I can think in peace. Thank you, I feel purified and at peace."

"I don't usually write like this, It is the first time that I've put all this on paper. It's well past midnight, but this feels so liberating, almost like painting. And I can say: It was worth writing this!"

"I guess I didn't answer any of your questions, but at least I felt relieved."

I thank from my heart all those who wrote to me. I only hope that this book reflects at least a tiny part of the philosophy of life that was evident in the books and articles I read, in people's comments, in various discussions and, last but not least, in the confidential letters I received. In all instances, I quote their words verbatim and have changed their names only to protect their anonymity.

Finally, I would like to thank my wife Katja for encouraging me to write about a subject which she knew had interested me for a long time.

FOREWORD
BY CHRIS IVESON

Ben Furman has written an important book and those who know his work will recognise his characteristic generosity of spirit. In this book he gives voice to three hundred stories of personal survival: Leena, Lassi, Hilkka, Riitta, Sirpa, Sari, Lisa, Kati, Ritva and many others, named and unnamed, are given a chance to speak of their strength and resilience in the face of deprivation and abuse.

A psychiatrist and internationally renowned solution-focused therapist, Ben has a passionate belief in the strengths and resources, however well they may be hidden or disguised, that each troubled person carries with them through life. He is a vocal opponent of all ideas and practices which support the automatic assumption that childhood experiences cause permanent damage, inevitably determining adult behaviour and of abuse creating abusers. Survivors have always known that a difficult past does not necessarily lead to a troubled future."

The book has arisen from Ben Furman's long-standing interest in how children survive abuse, his conversations with other professionals, his avid exploration of the literature and, most important of all, the three hundred letters he received following a magazine article. Yvonne Dolan, Brief Therapy's most inspiring writer on survival (*Resolving Sexual Abuse,*

Norton, 1991 and *One Small Step,* Papier-Mache, 1998), and an accomplished 'quilter' herself, would recognise the quilt-like quality of this book, made up of individual free-standing stories woven with Ben's own words into a patchwork of experience which creates a new whole. Each story is a testament to personal strength; the whole is a loudly voiced challenge to avoid determinism in our theories, our conversations with and about our clients and in the stories we tell of their lives through our case records. The stories tell of achievement despite deprivation, the ability to love, cherish and protect despite a childhood of abuse and rejection, adult happiness following childhood misery and of the deep sense of injustice which a failure to listen to these stories causes for those who have such stories to tell.

Ben also weaves into the 'quilt' (if quilts can be woven!) his own opinions and those of other colleagues from around the world who are interested in similar issues. His commitment to resource-based therapy helps highlight and value the stories of his correspondents and helps make sense of them from a more benign perspective than is often offered. His suggestions have a simplicity which makes them easily accessible and they carry no spurious 'professional' authority. His advice could be summarised thus: "This sometimes works. Here are some stories of people who tried it. Maybe it could work in some way for you!"

WHY THIS BOOK?

One day a big motorcycle glided past me on the street. The rider was wearing leather. He had a straggly beard and his long hair was poking out from under his helmet. The bike had a big windscreen, which had written on it in big 'stick-on' letters: It's never too late to have a happy childhood. At the time, I did not quite grasp the significance of the expression, but the inherent paradox amused me. At first it struck me as a humorous oxymoron, like the film title *Back to the Future*, but gradually I began to suspect it was a riddle that I had to solve.

I decided that whoever the person was who originally coined this phrase, he or she probably didn't mean that we ought to alter the truth, lie to ourselves, in order to fabricate a rose-tinted view of our unhappy past. The intention was surely also not to say that we should pretend to have had a happy childhood when we didn't, by sweeping the dust under the carpet and inventing positive experiences that we never had. I began to suspect that the phrase contained a profound message.

I had come across a similar saying when reading Dr. Milton H. Erickson, an American psychiatrist, who used to say: "A person knows the solution to his problem, he just doesn't know that he does." At first, I had also interpreted this as a rather glib witticism, but later, as I studied brief therapy in general and the solution-focused approach in particular, I realised that Dr. Erickson really meant what he said. He believed that deep in their hearts, people often know what might help them and that a therapist's job was to find ways to encourage that inner wisdom to emerge.

This book is a report on my attempt to find a satisfactory answer to the question: What does it mean to say that it's never too late to have a happy childhood?

ONE BENDS
BUT ONE DOES NOT BREAK

Western people live in a psychology-saturated culture, which shares a common belief that the cause of people's psychological problems lies in what happened to them in their past. This is why many of us try to trace the roots of our suffering back to our childhood. We have that been taught that the basic cause for our problems is that we were either lacking something or suffered traumatic experiences as children. Experts have explained that the first years of our life are crucial for our later life, and parents, especially mothers, have borne the heartless judgements of experts who cling to the same old dirge: all problems, from wetting one's bed to committing violent crime, stem from one's childhood. We encounter this psychological doctrine everywhere: in public, social and political debate, formal and informal discussions, talk shows, newspapers, expert literature and interviews, students' texts and magazine articles.

Few rational people would say that difficult childhood experiences leave no marks on us, or that the experience of damaging forces within our environment do not affect our growth and development. The relationship between today's problems and negative childhood experiences, however, may not be as obvious as we are accustomed to think. Does a difficult childhood necessarily lead to a problematical adulthood, or can a person survive well in spite of earlier trauma and unhappiness? How can one explain that many well-adjusted, healthy people seem to have had difficult childhoods, and, at the same time, many others struggling with serious adult problems have been relatively happy as children? Many people who have suffered a difficult childhood can have problems as adults, of course, but no one can say with certainty that childhood experiences have definitely and exclusively caused these problems.

Statistically, children who grow up in unfavourable circumstances – for example, in families with violence, serious alcoholism, or persistent mental problems – have a greater probability of suffering various problems later in life than children who have a relatively 'normal' childhood. However, correlation is not the same as cause. Instead of claiming that negative childhood experiences automatically cause problems in later life, statistics simply indicate risk. The simplistic and linear equations.

Child suffers difficult experiences = Child will inevitably have
    problems in the future;
    and
Adult has problems = Adult obviously had a difficult child-
    hood

begin to seem less convincing when seen in the light of research on children coping with adverse life experiences.

The best known study on survival is the longitudinal study that Emmy Werner and Ruth Smith conducted in Kauai, Hawaii. For more than thirty years, these cultural anthropologists tracked all islanders who were born in 1955. In their book *Vulnerable But Invincible*, published in the early 1980s, they showed how fewer than one out of every three high-risk children developed into confident, caring young adults by age 18. Two-thirds had problems and were categorised as high-risk adolescents. When the two original investigators re-examined the same material in the 1990s, they found that two-thirds of these high-risk adolescents had actually developed into successful adults by the age of 32. Thus, according to this comprehensive study, as many as three out of four with difficult childhoods eventually managed to cope well as they reached their mid-thirties.

Many other studies have recorded similar findings. A report on a study by researchers Renaud and Estress of the lives and childhoods of a hundred normal and successful American men, which appeared in the United States in the 1960s, showed that a majority of the men had experienced traumas that were at least as serious as the ones that psychiatry and psychotherapy usually consider as leading to mental disorders. The researchers concluded that those "one hundred men who, as a group, functioned at above average levels, and who were substantially free of psycho-neurotic and psychosomatic symptomatology, reported childhood histories containing seemingly as many 'traumatic events,' or 'pathogenic factors,' as we ordinarily elicit in history-taking interviews with psychiatric patients who are in varying degrees disabled by their symptoms."

Experience through a century of devastating wars has shown that people usually survive amazingly well the horrors of war as well as difficult family circumstances. Only some children whose parents are alcoholics start to drink when they are older and those whose parents suffer mental problems only rarely become mentally ill themselves. Only a small proportion of children who grow up in violent homes become violent themselves, and only a fraction of those who have endured sexual abuse during childhood behave similarly as adults.

Contrary to popular belief, these emotional and psychological problems that afflict children are not passed down to future generations according to the Mendelian laws of heredity. Childhood problems and unpleasant trials may increase the risk of similar or other problems in later life, but these misfortunes do not in themselves cause those problems.

Researchers Joan Kaufman and Edward Zigler have investigated the heredity patterns of childhood violence and sexual abuse. They show indisputably that the common belief that these problems inevitably pass themselves on to the next generations is a dangerous myth. They say: "Adults who've suffered violent treatment as children will hear over and over again during their life that they too are likely to batter their own children. Thus, in some cases, the phrase has become a self-fulfilling prophecy. At the same time many of those who have broken the circle of violence have started to feel that they must be walking time bombs." The two researchers also say that this widely-held and simple myth has made it more difficult to understand the reasons for family violence and has misled both child welfare authorities and social policy decision-makers.

Psychologist Ingrid Claezon has done long-term research on the survival of Swedish children whose parents use narcotics. In the preface to her book *Against All Odds*, she says that "Against all odds – or should one say, against all our prejudices – some of the children whose parents use intoxicants survive well during their childhood as well as adulthood."

Why then does one child seem to survive childhood trials and a lack of positive experiences much better than another child who faces similar harshness and deficits? Researchers have gradually become interested in this question too. A rash of publications, conferences and seminars addressing this topic of overcoming early life torment have recently appeared all over the world.

The word 'resilience' has come to describe the human being's ability to survive, recover and persevere against various obstacles and threats. Finnish researcher and child psychiatrist Eila Räsänen, for example, studied how well Finnish children had survived after being relocated to Sweden during World War II, experiencing years of separation from their parents. She observed that a majority of the 'war children' had, contrary to the generally held belief, survived their trials well. Many of them thought that they had even learned from their trials and that the difficulties had made them stronger rather than weaker.

Experts in psychology have traditionally attempted to solve the problem of human behaviour by searching for an answer to the question: "Why do we become the way we are?" The attempts to answer this question have produced an endless amount of information on risk factors and the circumstances that increase the probability of illness, deviant behaviour and various other problems. Investigators have studied all the possible dangers so closely that many people have started viewing life's journey as a daring walk in a minefield, while raising children is as risky as walking on thin ice. At the same time we have learned to see, and gradually also to accept, that even if we had an abundance of money we cannot root out all the potential risk factors from the world.

Suffering is part of growing up and even if we try to do our best to lessen our children's suffering, a great many of them will still face more or less traumatic experiences while growing up. The fact is that some children will always encounter an unreasonable amount of suffering and bad luck. We have come to the end of that road. We gain no further benefit from listing various childhood risk factors because even though we can try to lessen them, we cannot control the world entirely and eliminate them all. Thus, during the last decade, researchers have shifted their focus and have begun concentrating on the reverse question: "Why is it that we do not turn out the way one would expect?" They have started to consider the factors that protect us and help us to cope in spite of all our problems.

There is a popular saying which goes, "That which does not kill me makes me strong", but what is it that enables people to feel that they were made stronger rather than weaker by their difficult childhood circumstances? In one of his articles, Howard Goldstein, a respected American professor of social work, writes about his current work as he looks at how people tell their life stories. He studied a group of older people who had all grown up in the same children's home before World War II. Life in the children's home was hard and full of suffering. The staff were mostly untrained and resorted to terrible methods of upbringing based on physical punishment and hard religious bigotry. The children lived in poor circumstances at a time when there existed no such thing as public health care or social services.

Contrary to the generally held belief, these abused and abandoned youngsters grew up to become adults who have mostly survived well, perhaps even better than average. When interviewed for the qualitative study, they explained their success in various ways. Some said that difficult circumstances taught them how to take care of themselves. Some referred to the religious nature of their upbringing, which they believe, as they look back today, provided them with proper values. Some said that the difficulties awakened in them a will to show others that they could accomplish the same things other people can accomplish.

Professor Goldstein reported that among his interviewees there was only one person, Betty, in her sixties, who talked about her childhood in a bitter tone. But Betty had also succeeded in her life. She had been a teacher of disabled children. Her husband respected her greatly and, together, they were proud of their children, all of whom had succeeded well. In spite of all these obvious signs of achievement, Betty was bitter and angry when describing her life in the institution years ago and her abject feelings of loss concerning her time there. Professor Goldstein was puzzled by her reaction and asked her how then could she explain the fact that despite such a difficult past she had lived in a way that gave her every reason to be proud.

"She started to respond," Goldstein says, "and then paused, obviously reflecting on what she had just told me. A bit bewildered, she mentioned, almost out of context, that she had been seeing a therapist for a while. Her beloved father had died a few years before, and since that loss, which she felt so deeply, she had not been able to shake off some feelings of depression. Then she added, as a rather solemn response to my question: 'You know, I had never given much thought to my childhood in the home until I went into therapy. It had never seemed that important to me until my therapist asked me about my childhood. When I told her about the institution, my therapist got really upset and told me that I had the most pathological childhood she had ever heard of!' She thought for a moment, and then wistfully asked of no one, 'Was it?'"

Betty's case shows that although our childhood experiences undoubtedly have a great impact on us, we are not prisoners of our past. Professor Martin Seligman, who is a recognised researcher on optimism and the inventor of the 'learned helplessness' concept, has noted that "change is not only possible but inevitable also throughout adult life. So even if why we are what we are is a mystery, how to change ourselves is not. Repeating the same mistakes again and again is an invitation to change your life. The rest of the tapestry is not determined by what has been woven before. The weaver herself, blessed with knowledge and with freedom, can change – if not the material she must work with – the design of what comes next."

Some people when young find means and attitudes that help them survive childhood ordeals better than expected. But what stops one from doing later on in life what others managed to do as children? It might not be an easy endeavour, but it should not be impossible. One just has to learn to understand the code and the strokes for turning trials into victories.

ONE

THE MANY FACES OF SURVIVAL

"There is also this saying that I've often clung to. It goes something like this: those who are tried the most are loved the most. I think it's from the Bible, and it has often been my consolation."

— *Virpi*

"What do you think helped you survive a difficult childhood?" was the first question I asked my magazine readers in 1996. No one can ever know for certain, of course, which specific factors helped us survive certain difficulties, but a question inviting us to identify the survival factors can be useful. By pondering on this tantalising question, we can learn about the factors that enable a person to bend but not break.

In Western thinking, children have traditionally been regarded as fragile creatures who may easily be damaged early in their lives. When reading books on developmental psychology, one cannot help feeling that in order to become a mentally healthy individual, a child must have an ideal mother, an attentive father, and at least one brother or sister. But what is the origin of this impossible dream?

Thousands of children orphaned by World War II were placed into children's homes where they lived in miserable conditions. The children were properly fed, but no one took care of their needs for nurture and affection. Doctors observed that many of them became apathetic and started to waste away. Some of them died for no obvious medical reason. Child psychiatrist Renée Spitz investigated the phenomenon and started to call it 'anaclitic depression', arguing that the selective disturbance was due to maternal deprivation, i.e. separation of the child from its mother. Thus she laid the foundation for a doctrine that has governed Western psychology for years. According to Spitz, separation from one's mother is dangerous and destructive for a child's development.

Spitz was wrong. Anaclitic depression did not occur because a child became separated from its mother but because of the lack of care, nurture and affection which could have been provided by a substitute care giver. There were simply too many orphans after the war and the children's homes were too short-staffed to take proper care of each child's need for love and nurture. The human child is a survivor! A child can survive losses but without care, nurturing and affection a young human being will suffer in the same way as young animals who lose their mothers and receive no nursing from another animal, not even a member of another species. Rhesus monkeys fall ill if they are separated from their mothers when they are small and placed in a cage where their 'mother' is an iron contraption with two baby bottles attached to it. They start to behave in a grossly deviant manner or they die of infections and complications. Nourishment is not a sufficient prerequisite for monkeys and their human counterparts to survive. We are also dependent on interaction and touch.

Spitz's concept of anaclitic depression became a dominant doctrine of child psychiatry and from there it gradually found its way into our everyday thinking. We started to believe that the studies had 'shown' that separating a small child from its mother is always detrimental to the child's development. It did not, however, occur to us that nowadays children in similar situations are not usually placed in crowded institutions, but are fostered by someone who loves and cares about the child. No one, perhaps, can ever fully replace a natural mother, but whatever the other person may provide by way of caring and nurturing may well be adequate to ensure the normal development and growth of the child. Our lives do not turn on a single roll of the dice; orphans ,after all, turn into normal and happy people.

Other People

The fact that a child's parents may for whatever reason be unable to provide the child with a given experience may not be as critical to its development as we have been accustomed to think because the child will often have a chance to experience something similar in relationships with other people. A woman called Maarit writes to us about her mother, who suffered from long-term depression and could not become interested in her children's activities. But many other people who were important to Maarit and cared about her entered her life, such as her grandmother, a brother who was five years older, her godmother, her best friend's mother and three pen pals.

In psychology, the question of what helps people survive a difficult childhood has generated the concept of 'protective factors'. Researchers have tried to define which factors may protect a child from the negative influences of detrimental circumstances. No definitive explanation has yet been found, but researchers are in relative agreement that one protective factor is a good relationship with a person whom the child considers important.

If, for whatever reason, one parent of a child is unable to show affection, the child may form a close relationship with the other parent. If neither parent is able to fulfil this bond, children appear to have an interesting ability to identify and connect with substitute parental figures, through whom they can acquire experiences that their biological parents were unable to provide, if they are fortunate to select appropriate adults who do not exploit this vulnerability and neediness.

Aila, for example, grew up in a family of diplomats who travelled extensively and had little time for their children. If Aila had made out a list of all those benefits she missed out on in her relationship with her parents, she could have filled an exercise book. However, she was a good-natured child whom everyone liked and, as luck would have it, she had two godmothers, with whom she had warm and close relationships, a friendly violin teacher and two governesses who continued to be very important to her as an adult.

Aila is no exception. People who have little chance of getting what they want from one relationship are usually able to find what they need from another person. Father can substitute for mother and mother can substitute for father. Grandparents and other relatives are often able to love, admire and listen to a child when, for some reason, the biological parents cannot provide such love and attention.

"I had and I still have an extremely sweet godmother," writes Virpi, whose brother was seriously ill and took all her parents' attention when she was young. Virpi felt nothing more than a burden to her parents. "My godmother believed in me and I believed in her. Together we shed many tears but she was the one who gave me my happiest childhood memories."

Adele, an American therapist, shared her own traumatic

childhood memories in an Internet discussion, describing how she found a support family: "I must say that my 'family of choice' rather than my 'family of origin' has given me wings to fly beyond the limitations of my past. I learned early on to 'do it different' and went out and found another 'family'. This new family provided acceptance, support and unconditional love – all the things I needed to grow as a person. I guess it's like they helped me put 'wings' on my spirit, and since then it hasn't touched the ground!"

In her letter, Tiina tells how as a little girl she took care of her brothers and sisters because her mother was seriously ill and, in addition, how she had to cope with sexual harassment by her father. "I had a wise teacher at elementary school, she recalls. "She made me recite poems from the first Christmas recital onwards – and I did, with moist eyes, at the spring recital, on Mothers' Day, and on Independence Day ... Only a couple of years ago did I realise how this helped me gradually turn my shyness into boldness, and my introversion into aspiring optimism."

One should not underestimate the importance of peers in coping with all this trauma. Many letters emphasised the importance of close relationships with sisters, brothers and friends. Some told about close pen friends with whom they had established confidential relationships. "All over the country I have pen pals who listen to me and support me," writes a man who uses the pseudonym, "Discouraged as a child, happy as an adult".

Nature

Potentially vulnerable children do not rely only on other people for emotional support, and as adults they seem to possess an amazing skill at finding sources of strength from a variety of experiences. Pets, for example, belong to the list of important factors, although one may not always realise their significance at the time.

"We had a dog," one survivor writes. "I turned from ugly duckling if not into a beautiful swan, at least into a goose. The dog was important for everyone in the family. We didn't hug each other, but we did hug our dog."

Dogs, cats and other pets provide countless children with unselfish affection and understanding. Seija writes: "Since I'm very fond of animals and nature, they've played an important role in my life. Dogs in particular have won my heart."

For many people nature has provided a means of survival. The letters I received often emphasised how important the experience of observing and communing with nature had been.

Anna-Liisa, for example, who was ridiculed and cruelly punished both at home and at school, wrote that nature was not only a refuge but also a source of positive experiences for her. "When I was a bit older, I stayed in the forest as long as I could. I loved nature and its different aspects, as well as the change of seasons. All my beautiful childhood memories are connected with nature."

Many of us recall a special childhood spot, a sunny refuge perhaps, in the garden or out in the wild. It might have been a big rock on the beach or a hill where we liked to think and daydream. Likewise, the heroes and heroines of children's books often have a special place of refuge for when the going gets tough.

Imagination

People have an uncanny ability to create imaginative experiences that reality cannot offer them. When necessary, children can escape into the world of dreams and imagination as easily as the little girl in Lewis Carroll's *Alice In Wonderland*. In their imaginary safe haven, children can surround themselves with nice friends as well as kind and understanding adults. Authors, actors and other creative artists often explain in their biographies and interviews how they grew up in difficult circumstances. Could it be that during these solitary and perhaps frightening times, their imagination was sparked into action on their behalf in a way that benefited them in later life?

The imagination can help adults as well as troubled children to deal with their problems. People who have survived prison camps, torture or kidnapping often talk about how their imagination helped them maintain their sanity in hellish circumstances. The late Austrian psychiatrist Viktor Frankl described in his books how, while in a concentration camp, he benefited greatly from focusing on the future. He dreamt that one day he would be released and would write a book about his experiences. Based on his own experiences and observations, he developed a popular therapeutic method that he named logotherapy. One of the basic arguments of this approach is that our well-being is to a larger degree dependent on our view of the future than it is on our memories of the past.

Other people have discovered for themselves the beneficial effects of a vivid imagination early in their lives. Satu, now a grandmother of five, had an exceptionally difficult childhood. She says that her ability to escape into an imaginary world was extremely important to her. "As a three year old, I was a great dreamer. I was certain I was of royal descent, so it was pleasant sitting in the morning sun, touching the dewy grass with my feet and waiting for my prince. It made life seem much more cheerful."

Terrtu, who felt that her mother hated her and whose father used to grope her, says: "Psychologists have asked me whether I've had suicidal thoughts and wondered how I managed without them, but as a child I had a secret imaginary family who loved me and gave me what was missing from my home".

Lea, whose parents sent her to live with her grandmother in a different part of the country, recalls: "I've always had a rather vivid imagination. To my grandmother's annoyance, I made up games, talked to my reflection in the mirror, learned to read at five, and used to lie on a big rock looking at the clouds, singing aloud and talking to imaginary creatures."

Likewise Tiina, whose family suffered from alcoholism: "I guess my limitless imagination helped me to keep going. When I felt bad as a child my imagination took me far away. It helps me still and gives me hope when things are bad".

Reading and Writing

Many respondents mention that keeping a diary or writing journals or poems helped them.

"Writing saved me. As I wasn't allowed to talk much as a child, I created my own world that I escaped into. There the sun always shone, strawberries grew in the forest, and the waves of the sea gently rocked the boat in which I was hiding. Writing to me is a way out, an outlet, a mental cleaning up, my most loved hobby. When my writing is published, I always feel great joy, the feeling that I could do it." says Taina, who suffered serious and regular physical punishment as a child.

This comment by Virpi probably describes what many people feel: "I don't talk about my feelings to anybody, but I 'analyse' them on my own and write a diary. That's probably why I haven't 'lost it' yet."

Virpi grew up amidst violence. She saw her mother try to drown her brother, for example, and was with her in the car when her mother deliberately attempted to crash into a lorry. Virpi's mother attempted suicide five times, her stepfather tried to kill Virpi and her grandfather shot himself.

"I've been writing a diary for some twenty years," says Elisa, "and during that time I've felt an intense literary need for it. I also read a lot. It's probably been the best form of therapy for me because it's enabled me to concentrate on dealing with myself. It's been my lifelong dream to publish my autobiography when I'm eighty something, because I've really had such a strange life."

It has been known for a long time that writing has a therapeutic role but only recently has psychotherapy started to use it as a serious treatment. A simple but effective way to use writing as therapy is to ask patients to write a letter that they are not supposed to mail. If patients are bitter at someone whose behaviour has hurt them, for example, a therapist may ask them to write that person a letter. Patients may also choose to reply to their own letter. This kind of "internal correspondence" often helps people distance themselves from past events, making it easier for them to understand those events when they also see other people's points of view.

Many people with difficult childhoods are avid readers. Some prefer fiction, while others read books on popular psychology. Many consumers of psychology books say that reading these books has greatly helped them. For example, the author of the number one - best selling pop psychology book on childhood in my own country says that for him encountering the American 'inner child' and 'co-dependency' literature was a life-changing experience: "I devoured it. I felt as if, for the first time, someone had really understood what my life was about. I found an answer to a question that had bothered me my entire life."

Books and films and other forms of culture help people survive by raising difficult questions, touching upon sensitive subjects and showing that feelings and experiences that have seemed extremely private are in fact more common than they think. Books teach people to be tolerant by helping them understand themselves and other people better.

"Books have definitely helped me!" says a woman who calls herself 'Splinter', and who does not recall ever hearing a word of praise as a child. When she tried to tell her mother what she wanted to be when she grew up her mother just said, "I think you'll never amount to anything." This painful memory is typical of Splinter's childhood. "I used to read a lot. Books offered me consolation, taught me to understand and look at things from different viewpoints. Books were a mirror in which I reflected myself all the time. They helped me grow."

Riitta lived in a small house where she had to share a bed with her father, who often sexually abused her during the night. Books meant a lot to her, too. "I read about the upbringing of children, about psychology, and I also read the Bible. However, the Bible didn't help me as did the other books. It only oppressed me. Either I wasn't able to read it in the right way or it isn't well written. Viktor Frankl's *Man's Search for Meaning* made the biggest impression on me at that time. It started my growth. He had survived on pure hope, so I thought to myself I'll be damned if I can't become strong and get me a kind and reliable man when the time comes. Almost by coincidence I always found the right book, the one I needed at that moment. I started to believe that God would always slip the right book into my hand. And I still believe that."

Books have also provided many people with the entertainment necessary for them to forget their worries and troubles for a while: "I've always been an avid reader," says Raija, whose parents' bitter divorce was very difficult for her. "I lived and still live in an imaginary world of books and forget about tedious reality. My ability to forget has been a big factor in my survival. I want to wipe out the tedious things that I feel are too painful to be dug into."

Other Means

When we start to investigate the protective factors that help people survive, we soon realise that the list is inexhaustible. We have already mentioned other people, pets, nature, imagination, reading and writing, but the list goes on. Many children help themselves by throwing themselves into school work or a hobby such as sport, music, handiwork, games and boy scout or girl guide groups.

"Hobbies took my thoughts away from family problems," says Juhani, whose childhood coincided with World War II. My mind got a rest and my body felt less tense while I was playing sports. By drawing and painting I must have described my feelings with colours because I felt so relieved afterwards."

Sari's letter says: "At school and at college I did fairly well. It helped me internalise the feeling of 'being a good person.'" Many other people who have suffered difficult circumstances, but still succeed in life, probably feel the same.

Many who have undergone a difficult childhood say that

they were forced to stand on their own two feet and take responsibility for their lives at an early age. Some saved themselves by fleeing the nest when still young.

Markku recalls: "My father beat me all through my childhood. The last time he gave me a thrashing with a leather strap he was taking his heart medicine and cursing about how he'd give up the ghost because of me. As soon as school was over I ran away from home."

Certain characteristics and attitudes have proved useful in difficult circumstances. Being strong-willed, stubborn and goal-oriented, for example, can be extremely useful. Many respondents said that early on they wanted to show others that they could manage, which also helped them survive.

Ritva, for example, who lost her parents when young and whose foster mother often beat her, believes that her persistence and stubbornness helped her get where she is today. Paula believes that her survival is explained by her strong will. "I've always known what I wanted and tried to achieve my goals despite difficulties. My former boss once said, on giving me a new assignment, that he knew I'd stick to the job by clinging to it by my fingernails if necessary."

Iris used to wet her bed as a child and was often teased about it. Gradually she found a way to respond to it, which gave her strength. "For example, they might put snow in a basin and make me sit on it without my panties. Then all my younger brothers and sisters were told to gather around me to watch 'the pig in the family', 'piss-pants' – I had plenty of names. Or they might spread my bed sheets in a spot where the whole village could see what kind of a pig we had in the house. When I was accepted into secretarial college my mother said to me: 'What do you think you're going to do there, you can't even type with those big hands of yours.' I was determined to show them, and later even won a prize at the national typing championships."

Jaakko, a venerable 84-year-old, fought in three different wars. He is married with four children, ten grandchildren, and six great-grandchildren. He was abandoned as a child, and remembers: "I didn't have a home or any relatives, so the authorities put me up for auction, and I went to the lowest bidder. At school everyone called me 'public parasite'. I decided to work my guts out as an adult and show everyone I could manage on my own. And now it feels good to look back on the old times. There's enough there to write a book. I've worked hard all my life and now I'm satisfied with my life."

I am convinced that humour plays a larger role in human survival than we imagine. Many people say in their letters that humour is an important means of survival for them but they don't really explain how they use it. This is understandable: writing about dark humour is difficult. We feel greatly relieved if we get a chance to laugh at the painful experiences of the past with our brothers and sisters, for example, but these are private jokes which outsiders are not expected to understand.

When people are able to laugh at their own fate and see it in a tragi-comic rather than exclusively tragic light, they are freed from the shackles of the past. Through the ages people have joked about serious subjects and used black humour to counter their misfortunes. In Steven Spielberg's film, *Schindler's List*, which deals with the Holocaust, there is a scene in which a group of Jews stand in a circle in the dismal yard of the concentration camp telling each other jokes about life in the camp. The use of humour in that scene may have perplexed the audience, but for the people in the camp, joking this way was clearly an important means of daily survival.

As I acquainted myself with some of the literature on crisis therapy, catastrophe psychology and debriefing, I noticed that experts rarely present humour as a noteworthy or useful means of recovery. The man in the street, however, knows that finding the funny side is often the most effective way of overcoming a painful situation.

Taina sheds light on this approach when she recalls how she used to use humour to help herself and her children cope with her husband's alcoholism and violent behaviour. "I remember days when the kids and I were feeling low and worried about something. I sometimes went and danced in front of the big mirrors in our house. I jumped and made funny moves until it was absolutely impossible to go on. I also told the kids 'crazy' stories and together we did all kinds of funny stuff. These were our survival tactics. Although my kids are grown up now, they sometimes ask me to dance in front of the mirror and usually I do."

One shouldn't underestimate the role of religion in survival either. Countless people with difficult childhoods have reported that religious belief has given them faith and strength. Religion also provides friends with whom to talk about private matters, which some people would never discuss with professional helpers.

I have not placed much emphasis in this book on psychotherapy and psychological help in dealing with survival but this doesn't mean I do not respect the role of professional help. I just want to underline the fact that many other means of surviving exist and that survivors have discovered these on their own. Let's conclude by reading what 'Suffered but Survived' said about the important role of therapy in survival: "I had to deal with incest during my whole childhood. My mother caught my brother and me red-handed when I was 11, called me a whore and gave me a beating. My period was always strong but when I went to work it disappeared altogether. I was overstrained and put into a mental institution to get hormonal treatment, but I didn't dare tell them about my childhood. Afterwards I got married but it was childless, and ended in infidelity on his part. I was flat broke, living on social security, and suffering from insomnia. I did sheltered work and also helped at a home in the countryside until a couple of years ago when my whole life changed. I told a psychologist about my traumatic experiences. They cut down my medication and I got my period back. My relationship to men changed for the better and I became more energetic. At fifty I'm having the time of my life. I still can't understand why my mother thought I was to blame. However, my relationship to my mother is OK now. My childhood taught me to cope with the hardships of life but it also taught me not to keep things back. There's always someone who'll understand. Now my life is filled with work and love. It's as if I was finally walking on the sunny side of the street and enjoying every moment in this beautiful country. Instead of being bitter, I'm humble and thankful."

The question of what has helped us survive "in spite of everything" or "even this well", can be helpful in itself. As one of the letters says: "Someone should have asked that question earlier in my life because when thinking about the answer I noticed how many strengths I actually had."

Two

UNDERSTANDING HELPS

An old Buddhist tale:

"A long time ago in India there lived a young woman named Kisa Gotami. She met a young man whom she fell in love with and who also loved her. They married and soon had a son. They were very happy, watching their son grow. However, at the age of two, he suddenly fell ill and died. Kisa's world collapsed. She was overcome by grief so strong that she denied his death altogether. She wandered around, carrying her dead son in her arms and asking people desperately for a medicine that would cure him. Eventually, she found her way to the Buddha and asked him to cure her son. The Buddha looked at Kisa, then said with deep compassion: 'Yes, I will help you but I'll need a fistful of mustard seeds for that.' When Kisa told him that she was willing to do anything to get that fistful of mustard seeds for him, the Buddha added: 'Yet, the seeds must be from a house where no one has lost his or her child, spouse or parents. All the seeds have to be from a house that hasn't been visited by death.'

Kisa Gotami went from house to house, asking for mustard seeds, but in every house the reply was: 'We do have mustard seeds to give but there are fewer of us alive than dead.' Everyone had lost a father or a mother, a wife or a husband, a son or a daughter. Kisa visited many houses and learned many different stories of loss. After she had visited all the houses in the village, her eyes opened and she realised that no one is safe from loss and grief, that she wasn't alone. Her grief turned into compassion for all the other grieving people. Then she was able to grieve over the death of her son and bury his body."

The development of crisis and catastrophe psychology was an important step for psychology in the 1990s. It has helped us understand how people react to traumatic crises and how to encourage survival skills. In a shocking situation people don't know how to act, so they start to act by instinct. They do what they feel is best at that moment. Only afterwards do they begin to process the event and seek answers to questions such as:

- What really happened at that moment?
- Why did it happen the way it did?
- Whose fault was it?
- Could I have done something to stop what happened?
- What are people going to think about me now?

How people answer these and similar questions after an accident is critical to their survival. Crime victims, for example, benefit from understanding what happened and that they shouldn't blame themselves. They will also be helped by realising that they acted as rationally as possible considering the circumstances and by believing that they can recover.

Psychological first aid, or debriefing, is an essential part of crisis psychology. Immediately after a shocking event – often on the same or the following day – victims are offered support and a chance to talk and process the event.

Debriefing helps crisis victims distance themselves from the event and provides them with a chance to learn how others have reacted in similar situations, helping them understand themselves and others better. They become convinced that their reactions were normal and proper and realise that, with the knowledge and skills they had in that situation, they coul not have prevented the accident. The purpose of debriefing is to give victims the hope – however shocking the event - that they can survive it in the course of time.

A frightening and anxiety-provoking experience becomes less frightening as one starts to gain some distance and begins to understand what really happened and what it was all about. For example, how successfully children cope in families where parents have drink problems appears to depend less on how dreadful the experiences are than on whether the children had at the time a chance to ventilate their feelings with another person in a manner not dissimilar from debriefing. That person can be practically anybody - a family member, relative, godmother, support person or another child who has had similar problems with his or her family. Talking helps children distance themselves from their troubled family. They will not blame themselves and will learn to view their problems calmly and take them less personally.

"I knew my mother was an alcoholic," says Risto, "and my family often talked about it. She sometimes left us at home alone at night and go to a bar. And I remember the promises she made and broke. Of course I was always disappointed, but I knew she was an alcoholic and that's what alcoholics are like."

Only recently have experts realised how important it is for children to talk about their hardships and meet other children in similar positions. Meetings and conversation groups have been organised for children who have suffered from war, incest, physical abuse or alcoholic parents. Families that suffer from illnesses, disabilities or other problems can participate in adaptation training, through courses and camps that also offer the children a chance to get information and talk to others in similar situations. In the United States, adaptation training is used for supporting children whose parents suffer from long-term depression. Experts know that a depressed parent increases the risk of depression in children's later lives. Research on children brought up in depressed families and not suffering from depression themselves shows these children have recognised that the illness has nothing to do with them. This observation has prompted adaptation trainers to provide children of depressed families with explicit information on depression. The children are given an opportunity to ask questions and discuss all the matters that bother them as well as to meet other children. The results have been so encouraging that adaptation training is now offered to deal with other types of mental problems.

Ideally, feelings such as confusion, shame and guilt - related to shocking and negative experiences - should be processed in childhood. Yet it is never too late to start.

"My father was a real tyrant," Heli says of her childhood. "He was always in command. We weren't allowed to disagree with him. Every now and then he would have a serious fit of rage and his main target would be my mother. What I remember most clearly from those days is fear. It was terribly oppressive because as a kid I couldn't specify things, I couldn't understand what was happening and why. It was just tough and scary to be at home. I would have wanted to help my mother but my fear of my father was too great, to the extent of paralysing me. I remember hoping that my mother and father would get a divorce but they never did. Then my siblings and I grew up and flew the nest. As an adult I started to find out things that gave me a better picture of the past. I started to understand why he acted the way he did. I also started to realise that there was something good in him too, although it's usually easier to see the bad. I never managed to accept all the evil things I witnessed, but I've learned to understand some of the causes and effects of his behaviour."

There are many ways in which we can learn to understand our past. We can read about it, listen to experts, process the events on our own or discuss them with other people who have similar experiences.

Leila suffered from her mother's unpredictable behaviour as a child. She just couldn't understand her mother's moods: one moment she was happy and in good spirits, the next moment she was gloomy and angry. Leila could never tell what kind of mood her mother was going to be in, and she expended a lot of energy in trying to predict her reactions. As a teenager, she happened to read about manic-depressive illness (today known as *bipolar mood disorder*) in a magazine, and finally recognised her mother's condition. She went into the library and read all the books she could find on the subject. She realised what her mother's behaviour was about, and when, a couple of years later, she was taken into psychiatric care and diagnosed as manic-depressive, Leila knew she had been right all along.

Today there are many different conversation groups where people can swap experiences with others who have undergone similar hardships in their childhood. The best-known are co-dependency groups, which are targeted for adult children of alcoholic parents and which apply the teachings of Alcoholics Anonymous. The groups provide people who have suffered from their parents' alcoholism or other illnesses as children with an opportunity to discuss their experiences and continue their lives.

In recent years, many have found the Internet and e-mail

useful media to discuss private matters with other people. Internet news groups provide millions of people all over the world with a forum to discuss various subjects. The wide selection includes several groups where people discuss difficult childhood experiences, including abuse and survival. Those interested can browse and participate in groups whose addresses usually start with something like alt.abuse, alt.support or alt.recovery.

Leena, for example, found that processing her experiences with other people helped her understand her past better: "I've realised that we should learn from our hardships rather than just suffer. My insight regarding myself and others has increased. Now that I've forgiven my mother for all the wrongs I suffered, I can understand her better – she did what she could. In the end, I experienced my childhood ordeals in my own way. I grew up depressed, disheartened and feeling worthless. Someone else would have reacted differently, would have persevered and showed others that he or she could cope."

Her father's alcoholism was a heavy burden to Taru as a child but she too made a conscious attempt to understand her father: "At the moment I don't know how my father is doing. When he drinks, we don't keep in touch. But I miss him so much it hurts. I love him despite all he has done to me. It isn't always easy. He can't help being sick and I can't help it either. It took me a long time to realise this. I'm not his healer, I'm his daughter."

When children encounter subjects that are incomprehensible and perplexing, they become troubled. They may try to talk to adults, but if the subject seems touchy and improper for discussion at home or outside it, children process it alone, perhaps drawing incorrect conclusions. However, these conclusions can be corrected even years later if they discuss their past with other people. Pia, for example, whom I met several years ago when working in a psychiatric hospital, had long thought that her mother had abandoned her when she was little. There was bitterness in her voice as she uttered the fatal words: "My mother abandoned me when I was three." However, we managed to persuade her mother to visit the hospital and talk about Pia. During the meeting Pia's mother said she never thought she had abandoned her. She had had alcohol problems at that time and her life had been so messy that she had found it best to arrange a better home for Pia than she could offer herself. Social workers had helped her find a substitute family for Pia in another town. Pia's mother had mourned the loss of her daughter but stuck to her decision, thinking it would be best for Pia. Talking about the past and listening to her mother's point of view helped Pia understand her mother and form a more realistic picture of her own life.

Marjatta tells in her letter how her parents gave her to her mother's sister when she was three. "My older sister and my one-year-old twin brothers got to stay at home. I often wondered in my own mind why I was given away. My aunt told me that my family had been so poor that they couldn't afford to feed all the kids. This answer did not satisfy me because it didn't make sense. As an adult I wrote to my father to find out the real answer. He said that the real reason was that he had thought that I was not his child." The unpleasant truth satisfied Marjatta better than the dubious white lie she had been offered instead.

It may not be easy to initiate a conversation about childhood hardships with one's parents. If the parents have the slightest feeling of being blamed by their children, they may get defensive, so the conversation achieves nothing. People often tell me that when they attempt to talk about their childhood with their mother or father after psychotherapy, the consequences are catastrophic.

But when people manage to process their past on their own or with other people and then discuss it with their parents without any grudge, like curious historians, the results can prove extremely fruitful. The discussion may provide a thorough and honest picture of why their family was the way it was.

Tiina says that she has positive discussions with her parents. She grew up in an alcoholic home and was often teased by other children in her neighbourhood and at school. "I talked to my parents about the past and many things dawned on me. I'm not planning suicide any more and my nightmares stopped after I talked things straight with my father. In fact, I had a dream soon after our talk where I wasn't oppressed at all, but was surprised to find a doorstep I had been looking for in my dreams. I stepped in and looked around and nothing had changed. I felt peaceful and left. My nightmares stopped then and there."

Similarly, Raila managed to talk about her childhood with her mother. "I've learned to cope by talking to professional helpers but, strangely enough, also to my mother, who realises the pain she brought me even though she continues to booze it up with the same guy."

During the writing of this book, I took a taxi from Vienna airport to an international psychotherapy conference. I talked to the driver, who was from Yugoslavia, and mentioned my book. He got interested in the subject and told me how his father had often given him a beating.

"I always deserved it," he said. For instance, his father had beaten him because he had got his shoes wet while fishing by the nearby river. Then the taxi driver thought for a while and said: "Still, I'd never beat my own child."

"I wouldn't feel good about beating my child either," I replied.

"Then again, it used to be normal those days," he defended his father. "Times have changed. My father asked me some time ago if his beatings still troubled me. I just said that bringing up kids like that was common back then and nowadays they do it differently."

In the letters I received, many people tell how they learned to understand their parents over the years and even to feel compassion for them.

Minna tries to understand why her dead father had been an alcoholic. "My father was a musician. His family had to leave their house because of World War II several times. So, the starting point of his life wasn't very good. He was a sensitive man who couldn't turn failures into victories."

Saara writes: "It has started to dawn on me that my parents are just immature kids but who am I to judge? They never seem to grow up even though they are past middle age. It's just wonderful to know that their problems aren't my problems any more."

Leila, whose bigoted and extremely religious mother often physically abused her, says: "As an adult I've often pitied my mother for missing the joys of life because of her bigotry and religiosity. She is still alive and I've managed to 'educate' her a little and make her lose some of that narrow-mindedness."

Sometimes understanding their parents enables children to forgive them. Heidi had to deal with her father's sexual harassment and listen to her unhappy mother threaten to kill herself. Analysing her parents' actions has helped her forgive them: "As a young adult, when I had 'space' to think, I tried to understand my parents. I thought about my mother, whose own light-hearted mother gave her to my great grandmother to be brought up. I thought about my mother's childhood in a big family where she was, in fact, loved. But having no parents must have felt like a heavy load that she carried in her soul all her life. That much I can gather from her increasingly absent words. I thought about my father who was an orphan. Both his parents died of pneumonia when he was five and he had been in his godparents' care since he was three. I remember them and their daughters. I liked them but my father didn't. Being motherless and fatherless, his only memory of his mother is her dark shape in bed. After a few drinks he breaks down in sad longing. I realised that neither of them had parents from whom they could learn how to be a parent, that's why they couldn't do it ..."

A parent's serious illness or death often breaks the back of the bitterness accumulated in childhood.

"A few years ago I became seriously ill," writes Marja, whose childhood was overshadowed by her mother's secret and shameful alcoholism. "Before the operation, I wanted to sort out the 'facts of my life.' I forgave my mother. It was a big relief and it affected my whole life. I felt free, no matter what would happen. My relationship to life and my mother changed completely. Now I have the courage to live and to be myself."

Sari, whose father terrorised her whole family by his fits of anger, says in her letter: "My father died some time ago. I was devastated and I still am. I mourn him – feeling neither bitter nor regretful. Past is past. Nothing can be changed. So why fight back? I remember his good sides as well as his bad sides. I accept it. People talk about 'golden memories.' Perhaps my memories, too, will start to focus on the good as the days go by."

Riitta, whose father sexually abused her for many years, says: "I have built myself a life despite my difficult childhood. I've decided not to let my childhood destroy me or to let the old man have power over me. Yet I made peace with him. A least, I consider something that happened as a token of peace between my father and me. I went to our summer house on the anniversary of my father's death with my new partner, who is tender and loving. At the summer house, I had just planted my first-ever flowerbed (this my father used to do every summer) when a white dove landed by the flower bed, staying there the whole day. That night, sitting on the terrace we could still see the strange bird down by the flower bed. I consider it a dove of peace. Everything between me and that man is settled now. I visit my mother every now and then but we aren't close. I know that she did what she could. We just do what we can. I feel that if you hurt someone, it's because you yourself are suffering."

THREE

SURVIVOR'S PRIDE

One evening I was having a cup of tea with a friend of mine, a psychologist. We were sitting at his kitchen table with my three-year-old daughter wriggling on my lap. Suddenly she made a swinging movement with her hand, and my steaming hot cup of tea splashed on her. She was startled but before she even started to cry, my friend grabbed her in his arms, raced her to the bathroom, threw her into the bath and sprayed her with cold water. At that point, my daughter was crying at the top of her voice while I stared at the bathroom door with my open jaw in astonishment. My friend turned to me and said: "You probably want to take her now." I calmed my daughter down and helped her take off her wet clothes.

Soon we were back at the kitchen table talking about what had happened. My friend praised my daughter: "How clever you were, lifting your hands like that to protect your face from the hot tea." My daughter looked proud. Then my friend looked at me and continued: "And your dad calmed you down so well after I had sprayed cold water on you!" I was also shining with pride until I realised: "Wait a minute, *you* were the quick-witted one here. You had the brains to spray cold water on her so quickly." I thought I saw a pleased expression on his face but, at that moment he noticed how his eight-year-old son, who was also sitting at the table, looked a bit unhappy. My friend turned to his son and said: "And because you got out of

the way so fast, we were able to reach the bathroom so quickly."
Now the boy's face was shining too.

When we got home later that evening my daughter told her
mother proudly how cleverly she had acted when a cup of hot
tea had fallen on her. Her memory of how well she had
survived the event had become stronger than the memory of
how awful it had felt to be thrown into a cold shower after a
cup of hot tea had fallen on her.

A shocking event will create memories that have either
negative or positive effects on us. If our recollections are
connected with feelings of shame, guilt or anger, they can be a
burden. However, if connected with feelings of pride, those
memories can be a resource.

Catastrophe and crisis psychology has realised the significance of this fact. After a bank robbery, for example, it is
important that the staff has a chance to talk about what
happened immediately and that everyone present during the
robbery receives positive feedback. Everyone should be able to
think that their reactions were meaningful, or at least understandable and normal in the circumstances. They should
realise that each of them acted the best they could in that situation.

An American pioneer of the solution-focused therapy,
Insoo Kim Berg, says that therapists treating crisis victims
should focus on making victims aware of their own survival
methods. The goal is to make victims take pride in how reason-
ably and meaningfully they were able to act in a difficult
situation. Insoo tells about a client who called, begging to see
her immediately. Insoo promised to meet him the same day
and advised him on the phone: "During the meeting, be
prepared to tell me how you were able to survive this far."
When the client arrived, he explained how he had caught his

wife in bed with a strange man the night before.

"How did you act in that situation?" Insoo asked.

"I left the house," he said.

"How did you know that leaving the scene was the best thing to do?"

"I had to. Had I stayed, I could have been overcome with an urge to kill them both as well as myself."

"What did you do instead? What did you do after you left the house?"

"I wandered around the streets trying to get my act together."

"It was extremely sensible of you in that situation," replied Insoo. The conversation continued, Insoo asking questions and repeating how sensibly the client had acted in the stressful situation.

After a shocking event people often criticise their own actions and reactions. They may even reproach themselves directly for not having said this or that, or for not having been quick enough to do this instead of that.

People have difficulty in judging their own reactions and survival methods because of their natural tendency towards self-criticism. Often they need someone else to make them realise that the methods they chose were actually rather intelligent considering the circumstances.

"It's stupid of me not to have brought this up before," people who have held back something for years may say. But is this kind of self-criticism justified? How can they tell that it would have been better to talk about it sooner? Couldn't we rather say that they acted wisely? Perhaps they waited for the right moment to open up and were wise enough to wait until they were ready.

The central idea of crisis therapy – that of recognising the meaningfulness of one's reactions and attitudes – applies to us all when we look back on our responses to our childhood trials. It is often said that, when searching for a psychotherapist, people should choose carefully because sooner or later they will see their past through the eyes of the therapist. This must be true to some extent since, when discussing our experiences with other people, we can't stop their attitudes from affecting ours. Sometimes, for example, this will happen after seeing a film that you considered worthwhile and touching, but which may start to seem superficial and manipulative after a conversation with your cultured friends. Perhaps, before you start, you should ask your therapist: "How will I perceive my past after I've sorted it out with you?"

In recent years, psychotherapy has become interested in the so-called narrative approach. It regards people's lives as stories with useful narratives rather than as a series of facts, waiting to be analysed and explained. According to the narrative approach, therapy is not a means of finding out what has 'really' happened in the client's life, its causes and effects. Instead, it is a discussion in which the client and the therapist seek a narrative for the story of the client's life. The narrative should promote self-respect and hope without distorting the facts. The view mediated by the narrative approach of psychotherapy is comforting and optimistic – and this is the reason for its appeal not only among psychotherapists representing other approaches but also among philosophers, literary theorists and linguists.

In an Internet discussion group, Linda Metcalf, a therapist from Texas, describes how she helped her client see her past in a more positive light by using the narrative approach.

"Debbie had left home at age 14 to become a stripper to support herself. Her parents did nothing to stop or discourage her. Instead, they moved away without telling her and she was not able to locate them for several years. She was married at 16 to a frequent customer of the bar she danced at. Five years later, she is still married, with a 2-year-old. She came to counselling because of feeling guilty over her past and desiring 'more.'

"She told me she had dropped out of school in the eighth grade. After a few sessions, I looked at her and said: 'You know, I admire you. You strike me as a woman who wants more than a typical 21-year-old ... and, you are an incredible mother. You did what you needed at age 16 to survive. As you look over your past, if your beliefs changed about who you were then and you began to live within new beliefs for a few weeks, what would the significant others begin to see you do?'

'"They would see me with plans for a career some day, I would hold my head high and not slump down, and my daughter would see me in a respectable job that she could tell her friends about.' As she told me this, she sat up and held her daughter tenderly. We spent the last few minutes talking about what it was about her statement which made her sit up so tall. We finished by talking about what she did with her daughter currently that her daughter could tell her friends some day.

In two weeks she enrolled in an adult education class, her marriage improved and she told me in the next session that she had never thought about herself in a respectful way until that last hour. She glowed like the child who just received a gold star."

Linda Metcalf helped Debbie look at her past in a different light and take pride in her survival. That enabled her to turn her gaze from the past towards the opportunities for the future.

Our surroundings have a tremendous impact on how we

perceive our experiences. For example, victims of political persecution and torture may feel their lives are ruined while others consider themselves as heroes, depending on how they think other people perceive them.

The cruel and incomprehensible mass rape of Muslim women in former Yugoslavia is especially tragic because these women will always be considered as impure and unfit for marriage in Muslim culture. Their survival is made possible only by concealing the rape or changing people's attitudes, for example, by proclaiming the women martyrs and restoring their respectability that way.

Sexually abused children are usually examined carefully and put into psychotherapeutic treatment when the abuse is discovered. It does make a difference how this treatment is carried out. If badly planned, the treatment can increase children's feeling of being abnormal or damaged because of their experiences.

Among the experts focusing on this fact are Swedish child psychiatrist Lars Westerström and social worker Paula Heljestrand, who have developed the use of family therapy in the treatment of incest. They emphasise children's abilities to survive their ordeals, even sexual abuse, and encourage experts examining and treating these children to pay more attention to the survival methods children have discovered on their own. When children realise that their methods are respected, they start to respect themselves and take pride in their survival rather than feeling victimised.

Our past is a story we can tell ourselves in many different ways. By paying attention to methods that have helped us survive, we can start respecting ourselves and reminiscing about our difficult past with feelings of pride rather than regret.

FOUR

BETTER LATE THAN NEVER

If your childhood wasn't happy, you have all the more reason to try to secure for yourself a happy adulthood.

Petri had grown up without a father and always felt he lacked something. He thought he would never make a good father himself because he hadn't experienced a warm father-son relationship. He had married a woman he loved but did not want to have children, although she did, because he feared he would be a bad father.

Finally Petri talked to his friend Sami, who had never had a father either. Sami explained how he had had many father figures during his life. A sports coach, one of his mother's several boyfriends, a school teacher and many other friends had unknowingly acted as his father figures.

Sami's approach to being fatherless comforted Petri. He started thinking about men whom he had known and valued during his life. He realised that many of them had been, if not quite substitute fathers, at least targets of identification and even imitation. Gradually Petri started to believe that being fatherless wasn't as big a problem as he had imagined, and having children ceased to be an issue in his marriage. A year later, when his wife gave birth to their first-born, being a father didn't seem at all problematic to him any more.

The well-known English child psychiatrist Michael Rutter and his research group studied a group of almost 100 women who had grown up in London children's homes in difficult circumstances. The researchers wanted to know why many of these girls survived better than expected as adults. They concluded that positive experiences during childhood or later life protected the girls from the effects of negative experiences. Interviews with the now middle-aged women showed that many factors had protected them: positive experiences at school, the right husband, or a good relationship with their own children.

When I asked my question, "How have you acquired in your later life the experiences that you lacked as a child?", people mentioned many methods. One, however, surpassed others: the opportunity to acquire missing childhood experiences through one's own children.

Children and Spouses

"We can always continue to experience the joys of childhood by creating some child-like moments in our adulthood," Diana writes in an Internet discussion group. "We can appreciate moments of connecting with a child. We can enter a child's world. Sitting down on the floor to play a game of jacks with a five-year-old. Sharing the delight of a three-year-old who has just discovered how to smell a flower. Building a palace of wooden blocks - enjoying the crash as they tumble to the ground. Joining the thrill of a six-year-old who has just learned how to ride a bicycle. It's never too late to have fun with kids and extend your own childhood, happily."

Aino, who lost her parents and siblings in an accident when she was ten, says: "Now I'm a mother of three children who will soon be adults. I feel like a stable person nowadays. I'm grateful for each day, my children and the time I've spent with them. I now have what I once lost."

"Having a daughter helps me persevere," Riitta says. "She teaches me something new every day. I've learned to enjoy the little things with her. She has opened my eyes to the good and the beautiful in the world." Many women give credit to their husbands, thanking them for helping them enjoy an adult life despite difficulties in childhood. After having a father with a craving for liquor and a tendency to violence, finding a kind husband can feel like discovering gold.

"My husband has given me gifts I could never expect," writes Minna, whose father was a violent alcoholic. "I've been given a stable home with peace, constructive criticism and love. My husband is the best thing that has ever happened to me, as are my kids, my house and my friends."

Hanna, who suffered from her single mother's restless lifestyle as a child, tells how her husband's gentleness has given her what she lacked in her childhood. "During adulthood I've searched for safety and warmth, which I must have lacked as a child. Eight years ago I found my husband, who is stable and safe, and I can say that having an unbroken family still feels almost like a luxury."

Tuija was sexually abused by her father for several years. She also thanks her husband for her survival. "My period had started by the time I was 11, and my breasts were already large. I was teased for this at home as well as at school. I began to feel ashamed of my body, and especially my breasts. That's probably why I felt so wonderful at 40-something when I met my current partner and he told me how proud he felt walking around town beside a woman with such a fabulous bust! And I am proud to say that I enjoy sex. It's great!"

Other People

Although children and spouses are often considered the most important sources of positive experiences, other people in our surroundings can also offer us the experiences we lacked as children.

Kati, who suffered from her narrow-minded, religious upbringing, describes her mother-in-law: "She is like a mother to me, the opposite of my own mother. She is vain, emotional, and she likes dancing, using make-up and flirting with men even though she's 69!"

Liisa, whose relationship with her own mother is almost hostile, is full of praise for her mother-in-law: "I've tried to think what was wrong with me because I was never good enough for my mother. People close to me have warm ties with their mothers, so does my husband. I've been lucky to get such a nice mother-in-law. My mother's only sister, who is also my godmother, has also been like a mother to me."

"The greatest thing that happened to me after my parents' divorce was finding a boyfriend and getting to know his parents," writes Sanna, a student, who felt her parents' vicious divorce deeply. "His family is the one I never had. Everything is normal, not sick and crooked as in my family. His parents argue, but not because they've had a bottle of whiskey. I don't have to be afraid of fist fights. I don't have to call the police to come and get dad. His family is so normal and their family life is so wonderfully ordinary, something that I've always missed. I'm always welcome at their house and I feel like home. It's as if I had new parents and a new sister."

After reading all the letters I became convinced that people can still 'win the game' even though their life started out unhappily. An old saying, "Life gives us a fixed amount of happiness", gives people with an unhappy past reason to expect a happier future. Some people have to wait but will eventually get a chance to have their dreams come true.

Sari, now middle-aged, is finally enjoying the little things she couldn't even imagine having as a child. She lists "love, warmth, praise, talking, a big house where no one has to be scared and friends that are always welcome."

Hilkka felt unwanted by both her family and her peers as a child. She writes: "Unconsciously, perhaps, I chose a profession that gave me respect. I was only 24 when I got a bus driver's licence. It was relatively rare for women in those days. My job earned me approval and I think I was very suitable for the job. I used to get positive feedback from my boss and, most importantly, from my customers, who even gave me gifts."

Sirpa missed out on affection as a child but now she knows how to get it. "Sometimes when I'm feeling blue I'm almost aching for affection. Then I just go to my husband and children and ask for a tender hug. It gives me strength."

Ritva didn't have a father but now has many male friends. "Because I didn't have a father I now seek the friendship of older men. I've found many male friends at work and spend a lot of time outside work with them. For example, I have gone jogging with them for many years."

Riitta had to work hard as a child. One of her most unpleasant memories relates to the male travellers who often stayed the night at her house. She had to give them her bed and sleep somewhere else in the house. "As a child I always wished I had a place all to myself," she says. "I dreamt of a household with no men whatsoever in it. Now my dream has come true. I live alone and there are no men in my house. Oh, this happiness, Lin Yutang (the Chinese philosopher) would probably say."

Virve grew up in a violent, alcoholic family. Many of her

dreams never came true at the time, although she was always convinced that it would never be too late. "As a child I wanted to join the Brownies, take drawing lessons, eat fruit and stay at school. So later I went to senior high, business school, technical school and open university. I've also taken painting and pottery classes. And we eat a lot of fruit in our house ... It's as if everything I give to my daughter I give to myself."

A Talented Child

Parents of talented children often say they feel pressurised by their environment. They are told that they are taking away their children's childhood if they let them devote all their time to their hobbies. Well-meaning outsiders obviously feel that if children spend too much time playing the violin or looking at the stars through a telescope, they will miss important childhood experiences and regret it later.

It is a fact that children who practice an instrument or design computer software for hours on end are often left without the everyday experiences of their peers. But will their development be impaired by missing these experiences?

The traditional view is that talented children may become asocial if they aren't actively associating with their peers. However, the matter has been thoroughly examined over the years and nothing indicates that their social skills would be any worse than other children's, rather the opposite. Talented children usually succeed well and show above average social skills both at school and later in life.

Is it then totally harmless to 'lose' one's childhood? It depends on whom you ask. Adults who were talented as children often say that nothing has kept them from later enjoyment of the experiences others had as children. The actress Sally Field, for example, was once asked if she had suffered from starting her career so early and missing a normal childhood. She replied: "Sure, I missed a lot, but I just decided that anything I missed then, I would just have to do now." Adults can play too, and always learn something new about social relationships.

In an Internet discussion group, Ilkka talks openly about his childlike hobby: "I've kept all my teddy bears and bought some more. The total 'nosecount' is almost 200 now. Everyone has a name and a story, and I often talk to them, keeping a straight face. In a way they exist in their own world, which is very real and governed by a very symmetrical logic. The point is that I feel I can afford to be a bit weird this way, being still able to tell the difference between the two worlds."

Developmental Psychology

For a long time the psychoanalytic notion of child development has dominated the field of developmental psychology. According to this theory, children's psychological development proceeds through a series of predetermined stages that eventually lead to mature adulthood. 'Symbiosis', 'separation - individuation', 'oedipal' and 'anal' stages are but a few examples of the many phases which we should complete in correct order if we wish to acquire a healthy and wholesome personality. The core of the psychoanalytic theory rests on the belief that psychological problems are caused by disturbances in the development of personality at one stage or another.

Recently this deterministic model of human psychological development has been strongly criticised both within and outside psychoanalysis. People no longer believe in simplistic theories of personality which portray children as such fragile beings that their development is inevitably jeopardised if their mother (or primary care giver) makes the mistake of loving them too much or too little.

Instead, it has become increasingly understood that a child grows up as an integral part of its ecological environment, within a network of human beings that includes not only mother but several other people as well. There can be grandparents, various father figures, siblings, neighbours, nannies, friends, teachers. Contrary to conventional belief, children do not develop through a pre-set sequence of specific developmental stages. It is becoming increasingly obvious that the map that developmental psychology has drawn to describe the various stages of human development does not represent the reality. Children do not follow any fixed patterns in their development. Different children learn things in a different order and the delay in learning something until a later stage of development is not nearly as harmful as we have been led to believe. Children can acquire the experiences they missed at a certain age later on in their lives.

A human being is not a machine that has to be programmed in a certain way and in a particular order to make it work flawlessly. On the contrary, a human being is rather a flexible, ever-developing creature who can reach goals and learn new skills as long as its brain is going strong.

One of my Internet contacts, psychologist Linda Metcalf, is also convinced that it is never too late to acquire and enjoy experiences that we are expected to experience as children. She writes:

> "I don't think it's ever too late to have a happy childhood. I don't think we ever lose our childlike eyes, really. In fact, it's when we deny their curiosity and

desire for growth and learning that we become our troubled past. Then we allow it to lead us through troubled lives with excuses of why we 'can't.' ... Perhaps the key to a more fulfiling life may not be in searching for stress relievers, happiness or peace, but in placing ourselves in the environments that encourage childlike joy."

A story from a 'reliable source' tells about a man who happened to die young and was then taken to the gates of Heaven. When he met St. Peter he protested about having to leave the land of the living so early. St. Peter checked into the matter and noticed the man was right. He wasn't supposed to die yet, so St. Peter permitted him to continue living for the time being. The man demanded compensation for pain and suffering and, merciful as he was, St. Peter appointed him a guardian angel who would protect him for the rest of his life.

Satisfied, the man returned to the earth. He lived carelessly, knowing that his guardian angel was always somewhere near looking after him.

Once he was staying in a hotel when a fire broke out. Filled with a feeling of security he seated himself by the window sill to watch the fire brigade work. The ladder truck pulled under his window with a friendly looking fireman standing on the ladder. The fireman said to him: "Come out and step on the ladder, this is serious." The man was not worried and just said: "Don't you worry about me, go and save the others first." The fireman couldn't stay at one window for a long time. He shrugged his shoulders and went on to save the others, who were waving at their windows.

After a while the fireman returned with the ladder and told the man in a determined but friendly tone: "Come on out and

step on to the ladder, the building is going to fall down soon."
The man thought about his guardian angel and repeated:
"Don't you worry about me, just go and save the others first
and then come and get me."

Before the fireman could come and talk to him for the
third time, the building fell down and the man died. Soon he
was back at the gates of Heaven and even more furious than
before. He yelled at St. Peter: "What the devil is this? You
promised me a guardian angel but where the heck was he
when I was in that fire?"

St. Peter checked his files and documents carefully and
then said in his merciful tone: "According to our knowledge,
your guardian angel tried to save you twice but you refused his
help."

FIVE

AN OPPORTUNITY FOR GROWTH

One method of survival is an ability to see the good things our suffering brought into our lives.

"I'm no longer bitter because of my childhood. Instead, I think that it educated me because I had to cope on my own and with little money," says Anja, whose father was a violent alcoholic.

The pain caused by sickness, death, loss, crime and other misfortunes is partly relieved when we realise that our suffering has not been useless but has in some ways benefited us or other people. Accident victims, for example, often find consolation in the belief that their suffering can help other people avoid the same kind of accident.

The fact that suffering can also benefit people doesn't make suffering more justified or desirable. Neither does it free the person who caused it from responsibility. We can say that being involved in a car accident taught us something valuable about life but we can still demand punishment for the drunkard who crashed into our car. A broken bone may become even stronger after it has healed, but we shouldn't start breaking each others' bones or absolve all attackers from blame.

Riitta, whose parents were alcoholics, emphasises this

point: "Although I learned from my childhood, I'm not giving credit to my parents for it. I don't think I deserved a troubled childhood, and neither does anybody else."

My question, "What have you learned from your childhood?", is difficult to answer because we can't tell for certain whether our characteristics – both positive and negative – stem from our childhood. However, we have the right to speculate and make assumptions about where our characteristics originate.

In their letters, people 'blamed' their troubled childhoods for causing many of their positive qualities. They thought, for example, that their optimism, perseverance, cheerfulness, and their ability to enjoy little things as an adult and to understand other people exceptionally well all stemmed from their childhood traumas.

Jaana sees it this way: "I've tried to learn from my experiences and help others. I'm not blowing my own trumpet but people say that I have an ability to make others talk about their problems, or to sense their moods. They say I'm a very empathetic person. Maybe I am, then."

Elina's childhood was characterised by her father's drinking problem and her mother's depressive behaviour and several suicide attempts. She is also aware of possessing an unusual ability to understand other people: "Perhaps my childhood gave me a sixth sense. What I mean is that when people make passing but important and essential remarks about their life I might be the only one in the party who understands what they are talking about. Perhaps I have the skill to listen, to observe people and encourage them to say what's on their mind."

Maire, who is now 74, can see how life gives and takes. She lived in extreme poverty as a child and never had a father. She also suffered from a difficult rash, which made other children ridicule her and call her names. She says: "Those 30 excruciating years taught me how to be humble. They taught me to pity and understand everyone who's sick and suffering. When I meet mentally ill or disabled people, I never consider myself better than them. I will always be one of them. I don't think I'd feel this way if I had had a so-called normal childhood."

An American family therapist, Cloé Madanes, has developed a treatment programme for families with a history of sexual abuse. Abusers have to take responsibility for what they did and, among other things, apologise to the victim in front of other family members. Therapists also meet victims privately.

During these meetings therapists encourage victims to talk about the abuse, their feelings, fears and pain. Therapists empathise with the victims but also tell them that after experiencing something really bad, they develop a skill to feel compassion for other people, a capacity that raises them to a higher spiritual level and makes them understand other people's suffering better. Indeed, suffering does sometimes seem to refine people.

"At 56, I feel for the first time totally recovered from my past: the hunger, the whipping, the incest, the humiliation, the ridicule," writes Liisa, a mother of two, whose life changed at 25 when she found religion. "Now I can help other people and thank all those whom I met during my journey through many countries in the world."

"I'm proud of my difficult childhood and adolescence," says Leena, whose uncle sexually abused her when she was under 10 and who had to take care of her disabled siblings as a child. "I've seen the dark side of the street and after surviving it I feel very strong. I know more about life than those who've just been happy."

Mirja, who describes herself as an illegitimate child, left home at 15 after having suffered from her stepfather's advances, dirty talk and possessiveness. After talking to a nurse in a mental health agency, she says: "Now I know that it was his fault, not mine." When asked what her childhood taught her, she replies: "It has certainly taught me to take good care of my own children. They will definitely get a carefree childhood. I'll teach them to work and take responsibility. I'm involved in child welfare and animal protection organisations. I want the best for those who are the least able to get it."

Peggy Penn, a social worker and family therapist from New York, has worked with battered wives and their husbands for many years. She noticed that men who repeatedly battered their wives often told her they had suffered a disruptive childhood and were habitually beaten themselves. Penn believes that their background helps us understand why they became violent, but it doesn't mean we should forgive their behaviour. Nobody should defend their own violent behaviour by explaining they had a hurtful childhood. Penn says that she usually listens politely as the men tell their stories and then asks: "You've undergone a difficult childhood. What would you say, has it made you stronger or weaker as a person?" The men usually stop to think for a while and then answer: "Stronger."

Children who have been brought up in a violent home don't necessarily behave violently as adults. There are two sides to the story: although these children are given a negative example of problem-solving at home, they also learn how it feels to be battered and what the effects are. People who have been physically abused as children know especially well why it is so important to stop the violence.

As a child, Aulikki often witnessed her father hitting her

mother when he was drunk, and sometimes he threw the whole family out of the house into the freezing cold night. "Our family life was extremely violent but I didn't get traumatised nor did I become a juvenile delinquent. On the contrary, my early childhood experiences taught me to manage my own life differently. Now I have a six-month-old baby and a husband. He has the same kind of background. It goes without saying that we don't tolerate physical abuse in our family. Perhaps we do abuse each other emotionally sometimes, but I wouldn't consider it violence …"

Treating Children

Children's behavioural problems are often explained by their difficult childhood. When a little boy named Mika bites other children at the daycare centre, people will want to hear that he comes from a 'broken' home. However, it is a two-way street. The explanation may take away our feelings of confusion and helplessness, but it won't help us find ways to help Mika break his bad habit. By imagining that we understand Mika's behaviour, we start to expect less of Mika than other children. If we start to consider certain children 'disturbed', we will find it difficult to expect of them what we expect of 'healthy' children. I remember how, during my training, a family therapist encouraged a mother to set limits for her son's behaviour. The mother, who had internalised the above-mentioned attitude, put it in words: "But you can't beat someone who has already been beaten."

Explaining away inappropriate behaviour by childhood experiences can also be damaging because children themselves may adopt the view. A well-meaning attempt to understand turns into a disservice if children start to regard themselves as psychologically damaged, without any chance of successful life because of their past.

During my student years, I remember how a young boy named Markku was discussed in a treatment group meeting. An experienced instructor led the discussion, which focused on Markku's aggressive behaviour. It was explained in complex psychiatric jargon how Markku's aggressive behaviour was caused by his fear of abandonment, which in turn was caused by the many losses he had already experienced. Markku had been forced to move from foster home to institution and back five times during his early years.

This theory was watertight and explained Markku's behaviour well. Yet was it the most useful way of examining and understanding his life? As a student I didn't dare open my mouth; I simply protested to myself. Couldn't one also argue that Markku was in fact lucky to have been blessed with so many different homes during his childhood? He had been able to meet many different people who cared about him and tried to help him grow into a coping adult. I toyed with an idea of telling Markku: "I've had just one mother and one father but you've had many 'mothers' and many 'fathers.' Each of them must have taught you something valuable and given you something that may prove useful in your life."

I understood that Markku's life had not been easy, but I didn't understand why his experiences were seen in such a negative light in expert discussions. Was Markku a disturbed individual who had suffered several desertions and whose behaviour was a symptom of his fears, or was he a hard-boiled little wastrel, a young man of the world who would now have to learn self-control? It certainly isn't insignificant how we look at Markku and other young men like him.

'Wild Rose' does charity work in child welfare with

troubled families. She survived a difficult childhood herself and now enjoys doing important, fruitful work with children who suffer like she did. She writes: "I've learned from experience that, no matter how big the problems, children always have a chance, at any age, even as adults. This belief guides my work – no child is lost."

Timing

The ability to see the positive effects of suffering develops with the passage of time. For example, if your spouse suddenly told you he or she wanted a divorce, it wouldn't be easy to look at the positive effects of the divorce in the immediate aftermath. A would-be helpful friend who said at this point: "Think positive," might soon be an ex-friend.

However, the view may change as time goes by. All events, even tragic ones, tend to have both negative and positive consequences, and over the years the potential positive effects may become apparent. Parents who have lost a child know the depth of sadness that such a tragedy brings, but even they often say some years later that what happened to their family has changed their values and brought them something valuable about life and spirituality.

To be able to work out how we can benefit from suffering, we must start looking into the future, and ask whether the pain taught us something we would like to teach our children. Sometimes we must think further and ask: "If we told this story to our grandchildren one day, what would we hope they learned from it?"

It is well worth listening to elderly people, who are usually grateful instead of bitter, even if their lives have been filled with sorrow. Marita's story illustrates this. At 70, she feels she has survived relatively well despite her ordeals. She has had three demanding professions, each of which required training. She worked in each profession for more than ten years, and during the last thirty years she has been doing voluntary work helping other people.

Marita's mother died in childbirth. She had several siblings, and her father had to hire a housekeeper, who already had an illegitimate son, to take care of them. Marita's father and the housekeeper married within a year. Life in the new family was tough because the housekeeper's son acted violently, attacking Marita's father with a knife several times. Marita had just turned four when her father died and she was left in her stepmother's care. By then, her stepbrother had turned into a violent alcoholic who often threatened to kill her. At seven, she was so unhappy that she thought about committing suicide. She often cried, thinking she was the most hated and abandoned child in the world. After a couple of years, as if by miracle, she escaped her stepmother and was adopted by a respected and wealthy family.

But her new life wasn't always happy either. Marita was only 11 when a business acquaintance of her stepfather offered her a ride home and raped her on a remote forest road. Marita reported the attack at home although the man had threatened that something bad would happen to her if she did. Marita thinks her new parents must have believed her story because she never saw the man in their house again. At 17 Marita found a boyfriend, they got engaged and soon married. They had one child but the marriage ended in his accidental death at the age of 27. After recounting all this and a lot more, Marita ends her letter: "I've always been an optimist and a persistent person, I laugh a lot and I like people … As a young girl I realised that I could never ask people for more than what's been given to them."

Perhaps memories do eventually turn to gold. When we are old and wise, we can look back over our lives and ordeals with a feeling of gratitude. We may think like Tiina, the daughter of a violent, alcoholic father: "The road I've travelled has been very difficult and uneven indeed. It has made me believe in the saying, 'That which doesn't kill you will strengthen you.'"

Six

POSITIVE THINKING

There is an old Chinese tale about a penniless farmer who had only a small piece of land, a son and a horse. One day his horse ran away into the mountains. The villagers came to him and said: "Poor man. How unlucky you are, losing your only horse."

The man shook his head and said: "Don't say that. You never know whether your luck is bad or good."

After a while his horse returned with a herd of beautiful wild horses. When the villagers saw the horses, they said jealously: "Oh, how lucky you are, getting yourself so many gorgeous horses."

The old man shook his head again and said: "Don't say that. You never know whether your luck is good or bad."

The old man's son started to train the horses. One day, one of them managed to throw him off the saddle so that he broke his leg and had to stay at home in bed.

The villagers came to the farmer again and said: "Poor man. How unlucky you are, your son injured like that and not able to work at all."

Once again, the old man shook his head and said: "Don't say that. You never know whether your luck is bad or good."

Soon war broke out in the country and all the young men were ordered to join the army. The old man's son, who still couldn't walk, was the only one who didn't have to go to war …

There is also a story about two shoe merchants who went to Africa to find out whether they should start exporting shoes there. One of them returned home and said: "It was a useless trip. They don't even wear shoes there." After a couple of days the other merchant returned and told everyone enthusiastically: "What a great market potential we have down there!"

To be able to think positively means having the ability to perceive things in a useful way. We may have to look at things from many different angles to be able to find the one that will prove most useful.

As we look back to events in our lives, our thoughts about them will colour the way we feel about them. In today's social psychology this kind of hindsight is widely examined. Researchers have started to call it 'counterfactual thinking'. Basically it stands for all the 'ifs' that come to exist in people's lives.

The existence of these ifs in everybody's lives is natural. When someone is involved in a car accident, for example, their mind will be filled with ifs soon after. Ifs can be either negative or positive. Negative ifs add to people's suffering: "If I hadn't taken that road, this would never have happened." "If I had used the brakes sooner, I could have avoided the accident." Positive ifs lessen their suffering: "If I hadn't used the brakes at all, I could be dead now." "With less luck, I could have wrecked the car." "Fortunately, my insurance covers this." And in the worst case: "Fortunately, he died quickly and didn't have to suffer."

Similarly, our minds are filled with ifs about our childhood. The ifs are negative and make us regret our past when we say, for instance, "If it wasn't for my childhood, I would be happier now". The ifs are positive and increase our sense of well-being when we say: "If it wasn't for my childhood, I wouldn't be as wise as I am now."

Sari lost her beloved father at three and missed him deeply for many years. Her letter is a good example of positive ifs: "I often think that, had father lived, everything would be so different. I would probably not have gone out into the world – who knows, I might have turned into a sissy, a sweet little wife."

Everything Is Relative

Comparing one's negative experiences with the experiences of others is connected to ifs. During my internship in a psychiatric hospital, I used to ask patients who were about to leave what had helped them recover. I hoped they would give credit to the medication they received or the many forms of therapy offered by the hospital. However, many patients said that they had been helped most by the realisation that others might be worse off.

It usually doesn't comfort people if their suffering is compared with someone else's greater suffering. Each individual's personal suffering is always unique and comparing it with the suffering of others often feels belittling and insulting. Yet if people recognise that their suffering – irrespective of its depth – is, after all, relative in the history of mankind and the world, they can distance themselves from their own fate in a beneficial way.

In the previous chapter I wrote about the treatment developed by Cloé Madanes for incest victims and their families and the private discussions between the therapist and the sexually abused young clients that are part of the treatment. Madanes advises therapists to use the temporal perspective in these discussions. Therapists can explain to their clients that, although their experiences may feel absolutely excruciating at that moment, they make up a mere fraction of a whole human life. The abuse may have taken only a few minutes of each 24-hour day. There are 365 days in a year and many years in a human life. During the period the clients were sexually abused, there may have been many other important things happening in their lives. They may have had a stimulating spare time interest, such as music or sports. Therapists redirect their attention to the positive aspects of their life and help them set the abuse against that background as an unhappy event that will be forgotten with time.

Many of the letters I received provided evidence either directly or between the lines that the writer had learned this sense of proportion while dealing with that suffering.

Lassi, now retired, grew up in a poor, religious family, dominated by a cruel and strict father. He writes: "I was jealous of my school friends for having new boots that the municipal authorities had given to the poor. I had never had boots that nice. One day in town I saw a man who had lost his feet in the war, sitting on the bonnet of his car in front of a shop. He showed me how easily he could crawl behind the steering wheel using his hands and operate the controls to drive the car. He looked totally content as he headed off to his work. I looked at my boots, no longer displeased with them."

Marja was put into a religious children's home at three when her mother became mentally ill. Her relationship with her mother broke down, her father never came to visit her, and none of her relatives kept in touch with her either. Looking back on her life, she says: "As I was writing this letter, I started thinking whether my childhood was that difficult after all. Or is it just that memories become golden with time? Because each day you are reminded that today's kids feel bad, too. My motto is that what happened in my childhood wasn't my fault. I was just a kid, I couldn't have changed anything. Things just happened."

Eliisa's childhood was overshadowed by her mother's chronic illness, which required recurrent hospital treatment, and her father's alcoholism. Like Marja, she says: "No longer do I worry, feel pain and shame, nor do I pity myself. I don't think that others had it better than I did because when I hear similar stories I realise that they may have had it much worse than me. I've turned hardships into victories and learned to live better for them."

Granny, 72, who was sexually abused as a child and suffered a lot, writes: "... I have got over the worst of it now that I'm old and my children live their own lives without me intruding. I often go and nurse the old veterans who were wounded in World War II. They have both physical and mental injuries. I often think that my injuries are small compared to theirs. I have nothing to complain about, I have a roof over my head and food on the table. I'm not in the best of health but I can cope with it by living one day at a time."

The Future and the Past

It's natural to think that our past has an effect on how our future will turn out, but we rarely look at it the other way round. The future - that is what we think it will bring - determines what our past looks like.

When we are depressed, the clouds seem dark and so does our past: we have trouble finding anything good in it. Even if we try, we cannot summon any positive memories of our past. Yet when the world smiles at us and our future seems rosy – we may have fallen in love, secured a new job, or planned an interesting trip – our past also starts to look rosier. We seem to remember the good times that we had in our childhood, no matter how difficult it was. At the same time, our ordeals start to look like resources. Fortunately no one owns the future, and that gives us the right to dream and imagine ourselves a happy future. If in our imagination we let the sun shine into our future, its beams will light our present and past as well.

Minna was a close witness to her father's severe alcohol abuse for twenty years. Now that she is studying and relatively content with her life, she can see her father's good sides. "When my father was having a sober phase, he could often be a funny guy. He might make furniture for my doll's house, cook dinner or even sew. In other words, he could be a so-called good father."

Liisa, who as a child deeply suffered from her mother's violent behaviour, has also started to see something good in her mother: "Sometimes I remember how my mother praised and encouraged my sisters and me, wanting to be proud of us," she writes.

Timo has started to cope with his father's alcoholism as an adult. "My father had his moments. I remember how he sometimes relaxed after work, sitting in a rocking chair and humming a hymn. Then my brother and I would climb on his knee and he'd never push us a way."

Turning the Hourglass

People have a wonderful talent for seeing the ugliest memories in a positive light. Veterans of World War II, for example, who might emphasise their suffering and misery during the war, often tell us about their survival skills, perseverance, resourcefulness and use of humour in the war. In fact, most nations tend to rewrite their history this way because it strengthens their national identity and self-respect. Luckily, mothers often remember more vividly the happy moment of having their new-born in their arms than the prolonged pain they suffer during the birth.

"Now that I'm in my middle years, I look back on my child-hood with different eyes from when I was a young adult," writes Päivi, a 50-year-old divorcee and a happy mother of two. She is now convinced that how her past seems to her depends on how she chooses to look at it. "I can finally recognise the benefits of a troubled childhood that is full of shadows if I look at it from the shadow, and full of sunlight if I look at it from the sunlight." 'Poet' describes this metaphorically. "As I compared my life to an hourglass, I noticed that all my life had already flowed into the lower part. Then it occurred to me to turn the hourglass upside down: what had been negative changed into positive. Nowadays I look at negative things and see them positively. I've now turned the hourglass many times, and each time I look at my life flowing through the hourglass from a different standpoint, trying to be quick enough to solve the purpose of my life within the cycle of life. I'm like an old basket full of balls of yarn. Some of the balls are tightly wound, some loosely, some carelessly. In my mind I watch these balls of yarn, unwinding some, rewinding some, and some I've already used to knit a new purpose."

SEVEN

QUESTIONS AND ANSWERS

" 'Everything is relative,' Einstein said, as he was
cooking a clock and checking the time from an egg."

In this chapter I will briefly answer questions that I have often
been asked when I have lectured on the topic of the role of
childhood experiences in our lives.

Is being loved necessary for healthy development?

Everyone, children as well as adults, wants to feel loved, cared
about and valued. If people have experienced unhappiness
and disappointment in their childhood, they may feel that
they've never been loved by anyone. However, practically all of
us have had somebody in our lives who loved or cared about
us. But that somebody wasn't necessarily a parent or even a
relative.

Taina writes: "I was often very hungry because my mother
and father spent all their money on alcohol. I hardly ever got
food and when I did, I often threw up. However, in our apart-
ment building there lived a family who cared about me. They
fed me, and for a moment I knew how it felt to be safe and
cared about."

Many parents love their children deep in their hearts but
because of their problems they don't know how to show it.

How important is it then that children should have a close and loving relationship with their parents? Can they, without a lot of affection, grow up into normal adults? The Italian best-selling author Alberto Moravia answers a few interview questions in his autobiography:

– Was your relationship to your parents close or not?
– *No, it wasn't.*
– Not even to your mother?
– *Not in any way.*
– No affection?
– *Perhaps, but it didn't show.*
– So you were lacking affection?
– *Maybe. It's possible, but I didn't know it.*

The expression of affection between children and their parents is healthy and good for both sides but through the ages children have turned out well without it.

Why do some people refuse to talk about their difficult childhood?
There are many reasons but one of them is the fear of being labelled. This fear is partly justified. In Western culture it is a common belief that traumatic events during childhood damage people for life. In telling others about their ordeals people risk being regarded as deficient in some way and having their behaviour and character traits explained as origi-nating from their childhood. "It is one of the reasons I haven't discussed my ordeals with anyone," writes Teija. She is annoyed at the prejudice shown towards people who had difficult child-hoods. "People label you so easily and their idea of you is based on mere supposition. Keeping the secret is tough, but being labelled is even tougher."

Why do parents so often blame themselves for their children's problems?

This practice is very typical in Western cultures where the prevailing belief is that children are products of the way in which they are brought up by their parents. Of course, some children's problems are related to what takes place at home. For example, some children who hit other kids at pre-school may be spanked at home, and some children who fall asleep in class at school may not be able to sleep at night because of something going on at home, but these kinds of explanations are not automatically valid when children behave in problematic ways. Children can have problems for myriad reasons, and, as we all know, children can have various behaviour problems without any apparent reason at all. In fact, even when there are obvious problems at home, it cannot be routinely concluded that the child's problems are caused by the problems at home. It is worth reminding ourselves that almost all children manifest some psychological problems during their development – fears, nightmares, pains, tantrums, sleep or eating disorders, difficulties at school or with friends – and by and large these common problems are part and parcel of growing up and need not have much to do with the way in which the parents go about their business of bringing up the child.

What are the disadvantages of blaming parents for their children's problems?

The practice of automatically blaming parents for the behaviour problems of their children is often counterproductive in helping parents to deal with the children's problems, while also being a disservice to children. I remember from several years ago a case where a seven-year-old boy had formed the habit of refusing to go to the toilet and defecating in his pants instead.

A child psychiatrist had examined the family thoroughly and concluded that the problem was caused by problems within the parents' relationship. The parents believed the expert and tried their best to find ways of improving their relationship. Their relationship got better and better, but their son continued to soil his pants. When the family was seen at our clinic, it was concluded that it would be difficult to get the boy to learn to use the toilet without getting the parents to give up the idea that the problem was their fault. When the idea that the problem was a symptom of underlying family problems was questioned in an open discussion with the family, everyone, including the boy himself, started to come up with creative solutions to the problem. The mother proposed that the son should start taking care of his dirty laundry himself. The son suggested he be given some money each time he managed to defecate in the toilet. Both suggestions were put into practice and the boy got rid of his problem within weeks.

One mother told me how she used to suffer from her son's tantrums and sought help from experts. Her son used to throw himself on the ground and yell at the top of his voice. The mother had tried to locate the cause of the problem not only in herself but also in the boy's difficult birth, the birth of his little sister, his father's genes and his grandparents' permissiveness. The parents had discussed the matter with their son several times but it hadn't changed his behaviour. One day, as her son was just about to have another tantrum, the mother, as she put it, "just lost it." "Enough was enough," she said, "and without even thinking about it I suddenly told him: 'If you do it, I'll do it too.' Then I threw myself on the ground and started to shout and kick like he always did. He looked at me with his mouth wide open and said anxiously: 'Mum, don't!' and added: 'I'm ashamed of you!'" After that her son attempted to have tantrums a few times but stopped immediately when his mother looked him in the eyes and told him determinedly: "If you do it, I'll do it too."

When we think about what it is that we have done wrong, we can easily lose our ability to be helpful to our children in finding solutions to their problems. Children should have the right to stumble on the path of growing up; they should have the right to have their very own problems.

Young people often blame their parents for the difficulties they encounter in their lives. How should parents deal with this if they don't want to shoulder the blame?

Perhaps we should learn to deal with these accusations in the same ways George Clooney's father did in the TV series ER. George Clooney, playing the son, said to his father something like this: "I can't have a relationship or commit to a woman longer than six months, and it's all thanks to you!"

To which his father said: "I'll take credit for the mistakes I made during the first 18 years of your life, but what you do with the rest of your life ... that's up to you."

We should allow our children the right to complain about their upbringing. No parent is perfect, even though we try our best. We all make mistakes and there's nothing wrong in admitting it. When I sometimes criticised my mother during my youth, she used to smile and say, "I lack no faults." We should remember that Western youngsters are used to blaming their parents for their problems, this being a phase that usually passes if parents are patient enough to take it with a grain of salt.

Is divorce always harmful to children?

The disadvantages caused to children by their parents' divorce have been widely studied during recent decades, so an exhaustive answer would require a wide survey of the available research literature. During their early years, almost all studies on the effects of divorce on children were biased and purpose-oriented. They had been designed in such a way as to provide evidence to back the claim that children from 'broken homes' had more problems than other children. Information contrary to this prejudice – that so many children cope well despite divorce – was frequently ignored. When, for example, it was discovered that girls brought up by single mothers didn't have more problems than girls from 'unbroken' families, it was assumed that the girls must be damaged in a way that doesn't show externally.

Since then attitudes have changed. Nowadays researchers no longer focus on the simplistic question of whether divorce itself is harmful to children or not. It has become evident that the answer depends on myriad related things and factors. In the worst case a child can end up being a desperate go-between for her fighting parents, and in the best case she can have two lovely homes with caring families and many good friends in both of them. Luckily many of the researchers of today have become interested in finding out how people should handle their divorce in order for things to work out. This kind of research has already inspired many countries to provide counselling for divorcing couples. For example, in Norway there is a law which requires all divorcing couples with children to attend a few sessions of mediation in order to negotiate a contract that is good for the children.

The myth about the automatic detrimental influence of divorce makes parents feel guilty and may sometimes even harm children by making their parents prolong a dysfunc-tional relationship "for the sake of the children", even though everyone suffers from it. There is a story told among family therapists about a couple who came to see a lawyer to get a divorce. They were both already well over 80, so the lawyer sent them to a marriage counsellor for them to think it over once more. After the old couple had taken their seats with some difficulty and the marriage counsellor had discovered that they had been married for more than 50 years, she couldn't resist the temptation to ask: "Why now?" To this, the couple answered: "We decided when the kids were small that we wouldn't separate until all of them were in their graves!"

Do children develop lower self-esteem if they are never encouraged?

First of all, I would like to question the whole concept of 'self-esteem.' It is used today to explain all problems from shyness to criminal behaviour, from biting one's nails to unemployment. Often the explanation that a given problem is caused by lack of self-esteem only makes it more difficult to find solutions. Furthermore, self-esteem, or how much we respect ourselves, is not constant. It waxes and wanes with what goes on in our lives. The doctrine of self-esteem has it that our difficulties are caused by low self-esteem but one could just as well argue for the opposite: our low self-esteem is caused by the fact that we have difficulties. When people have problems, it is hard for them to value themselves. When problems are solved, they find it easier to respect themselves again.

I have begun to suspect that the constant talk about the connection of problems and low self-esteem has led many people to believe that they have a low self-esteem when in fact they don't. If we deliberately seek to find evidence of low self-esteem – whether in someone else or within ourselves – we are likely to find plenty of it. However, the opposite is also true. If we set out to look for evidence of good self-esteem we will find plenty of it. Self-esteem as a concept is misleading because all people both respect and don't respect themselves.

In former times both children and animals were trained by discipline. They were punished for undesirable behaviour by reprimands or beating. The world has changed in this aspect: now that we at least try to raise our children by praising and encouraging them. According to canine psychologists, you should never smack a dog in order to teach it to behave differently. Dog trainers of today tell us that dogs obey us much better if we stop punishing them for undesirable behaviour and start rewarding them for desirable behaviour instead.

Feeling valued and respected and getting at least some kind of encouragement from others are necessary conditions for human development. All people need to feel valued not only by themselves, but also by other people every now and then. I am convinced that if children don't get encouragement from their parents, they will go to find it somewhere else, from their grandparents, friends or wherever they can. According to the letters I received, even if you don't remember ever having been respected or encouraged as a child, it's not too late to have plenty of such experiences in adulthood.

Can children grow up normally without a father or father figure? There are many normative myths like this one in child upbringing and it is not easy to challenge them. People seem to believe in them no matter what the research says. Unfortunately, even scientific research on family issues has often been biased to support the idea of the cultural ideal, the nuclear family, while alternative family arrangements from the point of view of the problems they pose. But what we mean when we use the word 'family' has gradually begun to change. The nuclear family is just one of the many forms of families.

There are many other kinds of families out there: single-parent families, stepfamilies, multigenerational families, homosexual couples with or without children ... Each form of family has its pros and cons, and none should be judged to be worse than any other.

In the sixties and seventies many studies were conducted to show how sons of single mothers had more problems than those who grew up with a father. The results of these studies were quickly adopted as 'facts' although the only thing that had been found was that the percentage of children with problems was somewhat higher in the single-mother group than it was in the other group. The emphasis was not on the fact that in both groups most boys coped well.

Labelling certain forms of families as worse than others benefits no one. How well children from single-mother families cope depends on myriad factors: What is their relationship to their father? What is their relationship to their mother's new boyfriend? What is the relationship like between their mother and father after the divorce? What is the financial situation of the family? How does the children's environment react to their being fatherless? One could go on and on. We should keep in mind that, not so long ago, fatherless children were considered illegitimate and expected to be ashamed of themselves. If some of these boys have experienced difficulties in finding their place in the world, it may have been caused by society's prejudices rather than by the kind of family they grew up in.

Recent studies have actively discarded the myth of the necessity of having two parents – a mother and a father. According to studies, sons brought up by single mothers turn out as well as – in some respects even better than – those who have grown up with a father. The same applies to children brought up by homosexual couples. Society may condemn homosexual families, but the fact is that children from these families make it just as well as those from other kinds of families.

Why do so many parents verbally abuse their children?
In the old days parents often used to assault their children verbally. Unfortunately, many parents still do today. In the past parents must have believed that harsh criticism would benefit children's development: children would learn from it, or at least grow sufficiently thick skin to withstand verbal assaults later.

Many adults recall how their parents verbally abused them as children. They were called lazy, fat, stupid, crazy or selfish. Many innocent teenage girls were called whores just because they wanted to wear fashionable dresses and make-up.

Why do parents criticise their children? It's difficult to find a satisfactory answer to that question. When people who have experienced verbal abuse from their parents, ask of their parents about it, it is not uncommon for the parents to be puzzled. Some don't remember having done it. Others try to defend themselves by describing how difficult the time was for them or by explaining how they had had an even sterner upbringing themselves. In order for us to come to terms with verbal abuse by our parents, we may need to find an answer to the question of why they did it. The answer we give ourselves will have an impact on how we feel about the abuse. If we manage to make sense of it without blaming ourselves while at the same time also understanding our parents, it may help us not to take it personally.

An acquaintance of mine told me that as far back as he can remember his mother used to make belittling comments on his looks, such as: "You are not very good looking" or "How could anyone be interested in somebody who looks like you?"

He was an adult by the time he realised that several women had told him that he was handsome. He decided to take up the issue with his mother: "Why have you always nagged me about my looks?" he asked her.

"Have I done that?" said the mother.

"Yes, you have, often. I remember it like yesterday."

"Oh well, if I've told you that, it has probably been because I never wanted you to become as stuck up as your father," his mother explained.

How can people free themselves from the insults they were subjected to as children?

If children hear again and again that they are naughty, stupid, lazy, ugly or something similar, they may actually start to believe it, or at least they may start to fear that it may be true. While adults are sensitive to these kind of suggestions, children are even more so. For example if a child hears over and over again that he is clumsy and comparisons are made with his siblings, who happen to be exceptionally agile and handy, he may well start to acquire an identity of being exceptionally unskillful, even if this was not at all the case to begin with. On the other hand parents sometimes criticise their children deliberately, with the intention of helping the child learn something or to overcome a problem. A mother can tell her child: "You can't even put your clothes on by yourself, " meaning: "Show me that I'm wrong by putting your clothes on."

The French actress Jeanne Moreau described in a TV interview how her father used to encourage her in this paradoxical manner. For many years, Moreau's father disapproved vehemently of her acting. She had to leave home when her father discovered she had won her first role in a theatre production. But Moreau feels no resentment towards her father. Instead, she thanks him because by opposing her choices, her father gave her – even if inadvertently – the strength to make her dream come true.

Fortunately, it's never too late to question the insults one was subjected to as a child. In fact, many people take pleasure in being able to show that the person who mocked them was wrong: "See! You told me I was good for nothing. What do you say now?"

How does it affect children if they have to take care of their own parents?

Having to worry about their parents' health or survival is a heavy burden on children. I remember many years ago I saw a boy of seven years of age at the child psychiatric clinic where I worked. The boy had behaved strangely at school as well as at home. One of the many peculiar things he had done was one day to invite his friends over, whereupon they lit a small camp fire in the middle of the living room. When I talked with the exhausted mother, who was bringing up two wild boys alone, she told me that she was not only worried about her son but also about herself. Tears were pouring down her cheeks as she told me about her many illnesses. She feared that she would break under all the pressures she had to cope with. I asked the son if he was worried about his mother's health. He said yes and turned out to be quite motivated to talk with me about his mother. He revealed that he was afraid his mother would die of all the illnesses she was struggling with. I called the general practitioner who was treating the mother and explained the situation. The doctor came up with the idea that the boy could come in with the mother at her next appointment so that she could talk with him and explain to him that everything was under control and that there was no reason to be worried. We were also able get the mother some household help from the social services department. These simple interventions were enough to put the boy at ease.

If parents are mentally or physically ill, or if they use intoxicants, it is inevitable that children become concerned. They will feel greatly relieved if they can share their burden with an adult who manages to convince them that their parents will be professionally treated. The family approach is gradually becoming the norm in social welfare and health care, and more and more children are invited to take part in meetings where their parents' illnesses or other problems are discussed.

In one of the letters I received a woman describes her concern as a child about her asthmatic sister. The sister had suffered from serious asthma attacks and everyone in the family was constantly afraid that she would die. The only place where her sister could breathe was a rocking chair, which someone in the family had to rock at nights. The writer of the letter remembers how she used to rock the chair paralysed by the fear that if she fell asleep, her sister would die and it would be her fault.

Many people have come to know how nightmarish it is when a family member or a close friend repeatedly threatens to kill themselves. In such cases it is important that the needs of children are attended. The children need to be convinced that protecting their parents from suicide is not their job and that there are other adults who will take responsibility for dealing with the problem.

It should be pointed out, however, that being helpful to one's parents isn't automatically an intolerable burden to children. What seems to be more important is how heavy the burden on the child's shoulders is. Cloé Madanes, of the Washington Family Institute, says that children have a natural need and desire to help their families. She represents the view according to which professional helpers shouldn't deprive children of their right to help troubled parents. Instead of trying to remove children from the role of carer she recommends that children be coached to find ways of helping the parents that are appropriate to their age.

In an interview published in The Family Therapy Networker, Madanes describes how she used to help her father when she was a child. She says she is grateful to her father not only for all the love and care she received, but also for making it clear to her that he needed her and that she could be of help to him. Madanes says that her father went through some good times as well as bad, and when he was unhappy, he sought her company and allowed her to cheer him up, comfort him and talk him into a better mood. She concludes that by giving her the opportunity to be helpful to him, her father gave her a great gift.

How can children be helped to recover from a parent's death?

Tarja and her two sisters lost their mother when Tarja was 13. Nobody gave the children any emotional support at the time of the crisis. She writes: "I often wonder why, for example, our school nurse never brought it up. Losing a parent is always hard, even more so for children. We received some household help from the social services and we could have received financial support if my father had accepted it. However, rather than financial support, I think the authorities should provide children with emotional support in these kinds of situations."

In recent years the situation has improved tremendously. Professionals have been trained to offer crisis therapy for families faced with sudden death and there is an abundance of literature and audio-visual material to help children mourn and to coach care givers in supporting children in this process. What's most important in helping another person mourn is to respect the unique way in which he or she does it. There is no right or wrong way to mourn. One child may cry, another one may not show much emotion at all. One child may want to forget it quickly, another one may want to think about it day and night. Children have their unique ways of mourning and it is our job to help them do it their way.

It is often helpful for children, like adults, to think that even if the dead person will never come back, he or she continues to live in one sense or another. An image of a place where the dead person exists is helpful, as is the idea that he or she continues to act as a resource in the life of the child. In fact, psychologically speaking, people never die because they continue to exist as images in our minds. We can experience that the person we miss – wherever we picture him or her to be after death – continuing to guide and encourage us and to give us strength.

This idea has been useful to 'Sad at Heart', who lost her beloved father as a child. She writes: "My father's memory has been the most important resource in my life. His cheerful presence and deep love have provided me with a solid basis for coping in life."

How can children be helped to open up and talk about their problems?

As the saying goes, "You can take the horse to the river but you can't make it drink." The same applies to children: one can offer them an opportunity to talk about matters that bother them but one cannot and should not put pressure on them to do so. Ron Taffel, an American expert on parenting, advises parents to try less hard. He says that children like to talk about their problems with their parents but they want to choose the right moment themselves. Often when children spend time with their parents doing household chores, perhaps, or during a car drive, they spontaneously open up and talk about their problems.

Parents can direct smaller children to talk about suspected problems by telling them related stories and by reading them fairy tales that deal with similar subjects. Sharing your own experiences may also inspire children to talk. As another old saying has it, "If you want people to start talking about their brother, tell them about your own brother."

In our eagerness to get children to talk about their problems we should keep in mind, however, that even if talking is often helpful, children have many other ways of dealing with problems. They listen to stories, read books and see films that touch on the subjects that occupy their minds. They also have a marvellous ability to deal with things on a symbolic level in play and in fantasy. We should also remember that, if children do not want to talk about their difficulties today, they may do it tomorrow. And even if they do not talk with us, they will probably find a person to talk to sooner or later if they want to.

How can people liberate themselves from the shame caused by something they themselves have done or been involved with in their childhood or adolescence?

Many of us harbour memories of incidents involving so much shame that we prefer not to discuss them with other people. Shame is the fear that exposure would lead to other people looking down on us.

In order to free ourselves from the shame, we need to become convinced that such a fear of being despised by others is unwarranted. We have to change our expectation from "people will judge me" to "people will understand". After all, if we are often understanding towards other people when they tell us what they have done or been involved with, then why shouldn't they be understanding towards us too?

The best way to rid oneself of old shame is to speak about what happened to someone who is sympathetic. An understanding reaction along the lines of "I have experienced something similar myself" or "I think it's quite normal" or "It's more common than you think" or "It's not your fault" will often dissipate the shame. Sometimes exposing oneself by telling about the shameful incident is very difficult and therefore it may be advisable to do it in small steps. You may, for example, consider first discussing it anonymously on a telephone help line or on an Internet discussion group. And of course there is the much-used method of bringing the subject up in a vague manner: "What would you say if you discovered that somebody had ...?"

When we emphasise the fact that many people cope well despite their difficult childhoods, aren't we at the same time inflicting pressure and guilt on those people who haven't been able to cope quite as well, and who still suffer from the effects of childhood events?

I must confess that I haven't been able to find an adequate answer to this question. When people write and speak about the fact that difficult childhood experiences can have negative consequences, they mean well. They want to say that we can prevent many problems by improving our children's quality of life. Unfortunately, this important message may inadvertently create an impression that difficult childhood experiences automatically cause people to have problems in adult life.

On the other hand, when we write and speak about the fact that despite hardships people still survive, we mean well too. We want to make it known that a happy adulthood is perfectly possible for those who had an unhappy childhood. This message is important too but it may inadvertently create an impression that those who haven't coped well should blame themselves.

Both sides of the coin are important. Childhood adversities don't necessarily ruin the rest of people's lives. People can recover and learn how to deal with them, but this doesn't entitle anybody to belittle the suffering and the struggles that have befallen people with troubled childhoods.

Isn't the idea that people can survive anything and cope with anything a conservative political idea? Does it support the idea that we don't have to do anything to make the world a better place since everyone is the architect of his own fate?
Wayne Caron, a psychologist and family therapist, contemplates this question in an Internet discussion.

"In the US, a welfare reform act will throw millions of children into poverty. Thus, the messages that some folks grow up in terrible circumstances and do just fine seem to fit all too neatly into the myth of pulling oneself up by one's own bootstraps. Certainly there are resilient children ... but let's not lose track of those who struggle with the terrible effects of how they grew up. Let's not lose track of our obligations to the next generations."

He is right. We need to talk about how to survive ordeals in order to find ways to deal with adverse circumstances in life, but such discussions in no way free us from our social responsibility. Even if we realise that a human being is able to overcome almost anything, it is still our duty to work to improve the conditions in which people live and our children grow.

What is co-dependency and how does it position itself with regard to the teachings of this book?

Co-dependency, a concept developed by the Alcoholics Anonymous movement, was originally used to refer to the kind of behaviour of the spouse of an alcoholic person that enables the drinking person to continue the drinking pattern. It meant anything from buying alcohol to covering up the drinking from the rest of the family or the work place. The word 'co-dependent' was used to refer to a person who participates in maintaining the drinking pattern.

Gradually, the meaning of the concept was widened to include children who live in families where one or both parents have a drinking problem and who end up taking care of their parents. It was argued that such an experience damages children for life and causes them to develop into 'co-dependent' personalities who sacrifice themselves to attending to other people's needs while being blind to their own.

Co-dependency is not a recognised diagnostic psychiatric category. It is not an official disorder the way 'depression' or 'schizophrenia' are, but rather a shorthand for the increasingly popular belief according to which almost all our psychological and interpersonal problems stem from having grown up in a more or less dysfunctional family. The idea that we have problems because we are "adult children of dysfunctional families" has become quite fashionable throughout the Western world and many books on the topic have become international best-sellers. The idea has launched a world-wide movement which offers recovery from addictions and other symptoms supposedly caused by co-dependency. Liberation from co-dependency comes from reading relevant literature, acknowledging being co-dependent and attending self-help therapy groups based on the Twelve Steps programme of the AA movement.

The basic message sent out by the co-dependency idea is optimistic. It teaches us that, despite the possible damage caused by what happened to us in childhood, we can recover with the help of therapy.

The message of this book, however, is even more optimistic: therapy or self-help groups may be helpful to some, but are not always necessary. There are many roads to Rome, many alternative ways to cope with and survive the adversities we face in our lives.

How important is it to process childhood traumas in therapy?
Since Freud, it has been taken for granted within Western psychological thinking that working through past traumatic experiences is necessary for people who wish to be cured of their psychological problems. This notion has generated many schools of psychotherapy that focus in various ways on helping clients remember and process negative childhood experiences. Recall is assisted, for example, by hypnosis, interpretation of dreams, free association, breathing techniques and other exercises. Years ago I participated in a workshop where participants had to lie on the floor and keep shouting "Mum, don't leave me!" until they recalled a childhood moment of abandonment.

Pop psychology books often successfully persuade readers of the beneficial and curative effects of processing traumatic memories. Professionals within the field of mental health, however, usually have a more sceptical view. It may feel good to share one's childhood experiences with other people, but it is not something that has to happen in order for psychotherapy to be effective. Recent studies comparing the effectiveness of different forms of psychotherapy have clearly shown that the result of therapy has very little to do with whether childhood is discussed in the therapy or not. The kinds of therapy that focus on the now and the future, record equally good results as those that focus on the past.

Can processing childhood traumas be harmful?

By and large people benefit from having a chance to talk with other people about their past negative experiences. However, going to a therapist who concentrates on helping clients to recover repressed childhood traumas can be more damaging than beneficial.

Elisabeth Loftus writes in one of her articles about the tragic consequences such therapy can have. In the early 1990s it became possible in the State of Washington for crime victims to apply for compensation for therapy and hospital expenses. The Department of Labor and Industry (DLI) in Washington soon received an increasing number of compensation claims from people who had, after having undergone the kind of therapy focused on childhood traumas, recovered vivid memories and images of childhood sexual and ritual abuse. Since compensation claims were so numerous, the DLI decided to investigate the usefulness of this kind of treatment, by looking in detail at the first 30 applications.

The results of the investigation suggested strongly that this kind of therapy harmed rather than benefited the people. Of the 30 people studied, three had contemplated or attempted suicide before therapy, but after therapy the number had risen to more than 20. Only one person had slashed herself before therapy. After therapy, eight people had mutilated themselves. Two of the subjects had been in a psychiatric hospital before therapy, but after starting therapy eleven of them had been admitted to hospital at least once. Another alarming observation was that 25 of the 30 people were working and married before starting therapy, but after three years of therapy only three had a job and almost half of those previously married had now divorced.

The investigation didn't fulfil the requirements of a well designed scientific study with control groups and the like, but nevertheless it sends an important message. Therapy that focuses specifically on recovering childhood trauma may well be hazardous to your health.

Can therapy awaken false memories that are untrue?

Recent studies on human memory have shown that memory doesn't work like a video camera, which records events objectively. Memories change with time and people are even able to experience memory-like images about incidents that never took place. This phenomenon is used in hypnosis when subjects are told to regress into the past and to report experiences from earlier stages of their lives. Imagination becomes vivid in hypnosis and people are able to 'remember' how they felt in the womb, what it felt like to be born and even where they lived in a previous life. In hypnosis the mind produces very realistic and vivid images, which are easily taken for 'memories'.

If you go to a therapist who believes strongly that your problems are caused by repressed childhood trauma and that your recovery will be dependent on retrieving and processing these traumatic experiences; and if the therapist also favours the use of suggestive methods such as writing whatever comes into your mind, free association, dream analysis, guided imager, or hyperventilation, there is a high risk that you will start to 'remember' things that never actually took place.

Can people survive incest or sexual abuse without therapy?
A rather common belief held by experts in child psychology is that sexual abuse always causes serious damage to children and that psychotherapy is always required in these cases. More recently it has become evident, however, things that are more complex than that. Children are individuals and every case is unique. When in one child's case a course of psychotherapy might be a blessing, in another child's case something else might be better suited.

The latest studies support the view that children usually survive sexual abuse better than experts tend to expect. According to a rough estimate, when examined later, one third (20-40 per cent depending on the study) of victims of proven sexual abuse cope well and show no symptoms of mental disturbance.

People often think that in order to recover from sexual abuse, intensive long-term psychotherapy is necessary. In many cases this may be true but we should keep in mind that many children today are able to find the support they need from elsewhere. In a recent Swedish study, it was found that the majority of children who had overcome the experience had preferred confiding in family and friends rather than in professional helpers.

Can hypnosis or therapy make people see their past more positively?

In the 1940s, Milton H. Erickson (1901-1980), an American psychiatrist and pioneer of hypnosis, introduced an interesting therapy method that helps clients make their childhood memories more positive. The therapist hypnotises his client and asks her to go back in time to her childhood. In this so-called regression to an earlier stage in life the client has an experience of being a child which is so vivid that even her voice begins to sound like that of a child of particular age. Now the hypnotist-therapist takes the role of a wise and compassionate adult with whom the child can share her feelings and worries in the here-and-now. The therapist talks with the child at different ages, for example when the child is two years old, five years old, at primary school and as a teenager.

One of Erickson's case studies tells the story of a client named Mary. When regressed to the age of six she reported a traumatic incident. Her little sister had climbed fully clothed into a bath filled with water. She had tried to pull her sister out of the bath with the result that the sister had rolled under the water and nearly drowned. Mary shouted for her mother. The mother quickly came and grabbed the little sister, who was already turning blue. After a few taps on the back, she started coughing and survived. But the incident had apparently bothered Mary. Reporting the memory of having almost drowned her sister still evoked feelings of shame and anxiety and made her raise the matter in hypnosis while immersed in the phantasm of being six.

With tears in her eyes, little Mary told Dr. Erickson every detail of what had happened "the day before" and how her sister had fallen into the water. After listening to her story, Dr. Erickson started affirming the little Mary's course of action:

"You saw that your sister was in danger in that bath and you tried to get your mother to come to lift her out. When she didn't come, you were a smart enough girl to try and pull her out yourself. You couldn't help losing your grip because you didn't have enough strength but you acted cleverly in quickly calling your mother for help. That way you saved your sister from drowning." Little Mary felt better as soon as she saw the incident with new eyes. Erickson had several of these kinds of encounters with Mary at different stages of her life, comforting her and sympathising with her various painful or perplexing childhood experiences.

The case study and the book written about it, *The February Man*, have been the subject of lively discussion among psychotherapists as they seem to suggest that it may actually be possible for us to influence not only how our future will turn out, but also how our past presents itself to us.

How can I help another person recover from resentment or bitterness?

Letting go of resentment or bitterness brings many benefits. It produces an experience of relief while freeing energy and allowing one to direct one's vision towards the future. However, forgetting old grudges is easier said than done. It is made especially difficult by well-meaning friends who say things like: "Just forget it!" or "Let bygones be bygones." When people who feel that they have been wronged are expected or – even worse – told to forgive, they often feel insulted. They experience this expectation to forgive as criticism, as if they were being told that their resentment is out of proportion and that their reaction is exaggerated.

When helping people who are bitter, we should remember that the road to forgiveness – or getting over it, as some prefer to say – is long. Recovery from the experience of having been wronged is a process which consists of several stages and springing in one bound from the feeling of vengeful resentment to peaceful forgiveness is impossible to normal mortals.

When trying to help another person – or yourself for that matter - to overcome an old resentment, you may benefit from bearing in mind that working through bitterness consists of gradually developing a new understanding, a new view of what actually happened and why it happened. In constructing this new understanding you may find the following questions helpful:

– Would it help you if your wrong-doer admitted to what he did, acknowledged that it was wrong and showed some evidence of understanding how much pain he caused you by doing what he did?

– Would it help you if she truly repented and felt sorry for what she did to you? How would she have to present her apology in order for you to accept it?

– Would it help you if he was able to give an explanation as to why he did what he did? If this were to happen, what kind of explanation would make it easier for you to live with what happened?

– Would it help you if she was somehow able to convince you that what happened has taught her a lesson and that it has helped her change? What would convince you that such a change has actually taken place?

Sometimes life presents us with a chance to have a constructive conversation with the person who did us wrong. However, since usually we do not have the luxury of such a fruitful encounter, we had better learn to make the best of the inner dialogues that we can have with ourselves and with our wrong-doers.

What if the person who is the cause of resentment is now dead?
In these cases, writing a letter to the dead person is a useful method. In the letter, we can talk about our feelings openly and, if necessary, rewrite the letter until we are satisfied with it. Next, we can write an imagined reply to ourselves and rewrite it as well until we are satisfied. Giving feelings of resentment a verbal expression and turning that expression into a dialogue has proved to be an effective method of coming to terms with old resentments.

What if we are bitter at nobody in particular but at fate in general?

When the quality of your life improves, for any reason, the degree of your bitterness tends to lessen irrespective of what it is that happened to you in the past. For example, the resentment felt by many women and men after divorce often diminishes remarkably when they find new love. When helping people embittered not by the actions of a particular person but by life in general, it may be useful to focus their attention on the future by asking them questions such as: "What good things would need to happen in your life in order for you to be able to put the bad things that have happened behind you?" or "How could your fate compensate you for all your suffering?"

What causes people's problems if it isn't their childhood experiences?
We are so used to resorting to the theory of the bad childhood in explaining our problems that when it is questioned, we feel for a moment as if the rug has been pulled from beneath our feet. The truth is that nobody knows for certain where our problems come from. A plethora of academic traditions

ranging from psychology to the study of animal behaviour and from sociology to brain research have all provided a multitude of theories to explain why we behave in the particular ways that we do.

The causes for problematic behaviour are numerous and anything but straightforward. Finding out why a person behaves in certain a way in a given situation is practically impossible, and no single model of explanation does justice to the complexity of the human behaviour. Ultimately, we may have to accept this uncertainty. Even at best, our explanations are merely presumptions, hypotheses and theories. However, it may be comforting to know that 'knowing' the cause of a given problem behaviour is rarely a prerequisite for finding fruitful ways to deal with it and that a presumed understanding of the cause of that behaviour may in fact sometimes be more harmful than helpful.

CLOSING WORDS

"Success has many fathers, but failure is an orphan."

Old proverb

The question of "to what extent our childhood circumstances affect our lives and development" has troubled Western man since Freud presented his psychoanalytical doctrine at the beginning of the century. It's a question that concerns us all because it touches upon the basic dilemma of philosophy: Do people have free will or are they victims of their circumstances?

A group of students once visited a Zen master to hear him discussing this question. The master spoke about the dilemma of free will but the students felt they hadn't received an answer to their question. After the lecture one of the students asked: "Childhood experiences have a crucial effect on what will become of a person, don't they?"

The master smiled and nodded his head: "You're right. You're right."

Another student asked: "But isn't it rather that a person can, irrespective of his past, determine by himself what becomes of himself?" The master kept on smiling and nodding his head: "You're right. You're right."

A third student couldn't resist the temptation to comment: "But aren't you, master, contradicting yourself when you agree with both of them even though they're opposing each other?"

The master thought about this for a while and then said with a friendly smile on his face: "You're right. You too are right."

The question of how our childhood affects us may be more complex than we have been accustomed to think. Past experiences certainly affect us, but not in any straightforward way. A human being is not a billiard ball, whose reaction to a collision can be mathematically calculated. A human being is rather like a dog hit on the head by a stick thrown by someone. The dog may leap up at the person who threw the stick, or it may run away, or stay still and whine, or think that the person wants to play with it. Its reaction depends on many factors.

We can't change history - events in the past that have actually happened. We can't erase what has happened or undo what we've done, yet we can – to a surprisingly high degree – influence the way we perceive past events and what they mean to us. The past is not just a chronicle, a recording of what has happened in a chronological order. It's a story that's alive and changing as it's being retold, given new emphases, meanings, explanations and consequences.

A story tells how an old rabbi, who was known to be a wise man, arrived in a village. A young rabbi in the village felt his opportunity had come. The old rabbi was supposed to give a lecture in the village the following morning and the young rabbi decided to the test the old rabbi. He would approach the old rabbi at a suitable point during the lecture with a small bird in his hand. Then he would ask him: "Dear rabbi, I have a bird in my hand. Can you tell if it's alive or not?" If the rabbi answered: "It's alive," the young man would easily squeeze the bird to death without anyone noticing and then show everyone that the old rabbi was wrong. On the other hand, if he answered: "It's dead," the young man would set the bird free and show everyone that he was wiser and wittier than the old rabbi.

The following day, as the rabbi was talking to the villagers, the young man rose and challenged the rabbi by asking: "Rabbi, we all know that you are a clever and wise man but can you tell whether this bird in my hand is alive or not?"

The rabbi was silent for a moment. Then, with a mischievous smile on his face, he answered gently: "It's up to you, my dear friend. It's completely up to you."

We have every chance of having a better future irrespective of what our past is like or what our life at the moment looks like. We can't determine our fate, just as we can't determine which way the river will flow, but we can promote development and redirect the flow by preparing the soil for positive changes.

As I tried to gather the wisdom that I considered clearly visible in all the material I had – letters, discussions and scientific literature – I came up with a list of thoughts and guiding principles. I hope that they reflect the philosophy of life that this project has taught me and that they may be helpful for you in your quest for an answer to the perennial question of how we might be able to improve the quality of our lives through our own attitudes:

– Respect yourself for the many different ways in which you have coped with and survived the adversities of your life.

– Consider the experiences you have faced as ordeals that may have played a role in the development of your positive qualities.

- Pay attention to both your internal and external resources because there are probably many more than you are aware of.

- Be proud of your progress and your success and notice the signs that indicate to you that you're on the right track.

- Remain aware of what you want from life and the future. Wishes have a tendency to come true but no wind favours a ship without a destination.

- Believe in your right to have a good future. The harder your past has been, the more you deserve in the future.

- Have mercy on yourself and remember that you're not alone: it's always worth continuing to look for mustard seeds, even if you haven't found any yet.

Appendix

In order for you to get an idea of what kind of letters I received from the people who answered my three questions, I have reproduced here an example in full.

My childhood was actually quite happy despite all the anxiety, sorrow and crying. Of course I didn't feel happy back then; I was so anxious that I threw up at school, couldn't learn maths, and felt too ashamed to bring home new friends because my parents were drinking. The feelings of shame and anxiety governed my childhood and even my teenage years to some extent. My mum and dad were already drinking by the time my younger sister and I were born. While expecting me, my mum had been drinking and smoking cigarettes so heavily that, as a new-born baby, I suffered from withdrawal symptoms. When my sister and I were just babies, my mum used to leave us in our granny's care so that she could carry on with her carefree and irresponsible way of life. Everyone in the neighbourhood knew that our house was a regular boozing hole. My grandpa had been drinking and quarrelling with the neighbours for years. He was a peculiar man, who hardly said a word when sober, but when drinking he'd lose his temper over the smallest thing – so you had to be on your toes all the time. My granny couldn't even wash the dishes without him coming into the kitchen, yelling and shaking his fists. Yet he never hit my granny or anyone else; he just yelled and looked scary. But my mum was hit – by my dad and other men. She was often bruised and battered. Over the years, she lost bunches of hair and even a few teeth. Distressed and worried, my sister and I often listened to the sounds of mum and dad, or some other man, fighting upstairs. Staying downstairs with our granny, we could hear the sounds of breaking glass and furniture, and mum screaming terribly. Sometimes she would fall down the stairs because some man pushed her. She lived in her parents' house for several years before granny and grandpa got sick of listening to the noise of drunken guests. Even the neighbours complained.

My childhood was full of drunken people, yelling, fear, anxiety, and even violence, although nobody ever hit my sister and me. Were it not for our granny, we would have been put in a children's home. She was a pillar of strength that stood her husband's drinking and tyranny for years, and then took care of her daughter's children. She cleaned, did the laundry, cooked wholesome meals every day, gave money to everyone, and catered to our basic needs more than adequately. She worked like a slave and sacrificed her whole life, serving others. Even today, my mum asks her for money, and she cannot say no. I really pity my granny. She is a good, strong woman but over the years has become bitter and hard. She deserved a happier old age.

My dad hanged himself when I was twelve. Everyone talked about it and I became even more troubled and ashamed. My friends at school called my mum a whore and everyone could hear what they were saying. I thought I could never amount to anything because my family was like that. I often cried and thought about my dad, whom I didn't even know well. My sister was wilder than me, and she seemed to have it easier. I was the one who reacted sensitively to everything and felt the responsibility. Gradually I started to realise that it wasn't my fault that my parents were drinking. Instead of hating my mum or my grandpa, I started feeling sorry for them. They were what they were, and I was what I was.

I have always had, since I was little, good friends with whom I can share everything. I spent a lot of time with my friends as a child, especially with Rita, whose house was a kind of surrogate home to me. Rita is still one of my best friends. By the age of five, I was lucky enough to have found soul sisters, with whom I could invent imaginative games and grow as a person. We played a lot outside, drew pictures and made up different fairy tales. I experienced my happiest childhood moments while playing in nature, inventing creative games, drawing, reading and writing. I started to write poems and stories already at nine, and I still write. Because of all that creativity and play of imagination, I can say that my childhood was happy, even though it was also full of grief and suffering. Despite all her troubles, my granny too was often funny and had a warm sense of humour. She wouldn't have survived without her optimistic and positive personality; neither would I.

Up to my teenage years, I was shy and anxious in large groups, especially at school. I lacked self-confidence and was frightened that everyone could see what kind of a family I had. I never told anything about my family to strangers. I was certain that people would label me somehow if they knew. Then I became interested in dancing and turned out to be good at it. I made swift progress and performed in front of an audience, even though I was scared to death at first. Through dancing, I got to know myself better and gained heaps of self-confidence. I really knew how to do it, and enjoyed doing my own choreography and planning shows with my friends. I did better and better at school, and became less shy and troubled. It was as if an ugly duckling were finally turning into a beautiful swan. I realised that I wouldn't have to become an alcoholic or a loser as my parents had, and that I could do anything I wanted with my life. Dancing became my life, and I even became more popular, a bit of a social success, because of my skills and achievements. In addition to friends and writing, dancing became a form of therapy to me. I graduated with top grades, and was admitted to the Academy of Dramatic Art at eighteen to study modern dance. It was an exciting, happy time. I knew I had survived the worst of it, although I still had to face the fears and challenges of becoming an independent adult.

Dancing really was a form of therapy to me, because I decided to drop out of the academy during the first year. Instead, I studied to become an occupational therapist and have also studied dance therapy. Even though we were poor and I never had any real parents,

I wouldn't want to change my childhood even if I could. Despite all the troubles, I can say that my childhood was happy. I enjoyed the good moments outside the home because I knew that at home things wouldn't probably be like that. I'm happy for the fact that already as a child I knew how to express my thoughts and feelings on paper and in other creative forms. Without my difficult childhood, I might not have grown into the creative, sensitive and clear-sighted person I am now. In my work as an occupational therapist specialising in children, sensitivity and keen-sightedness are just the characteristics I need. I can sense fear and anxiety from a mile away. I have also learnt to be grateful. During my childhood, I felt grateful for my granny who took care of us, even though she didn't have to. I'm also grateful that my sister and I grew up as independent adults standing on our own feet. I have learnt that nothing in this life can be taken for granted, not even love, so you should feel grateful for each day that goes well. I think that my childhood experiences left me with such an elementary strength that I cannot be broken easily. I feel that I gain more of this strength every day, and I am glad to possess something of which I can give to others too.

Today I'm in a wonderful relationship that allows me to be myself. This relationship has enabled me to experience the love and tenderness that was lacking in my childhood. I feel immensely thankful for having been able to get so much love, joy and happiness during my adulthood. Even if it were to end now, I would be able to draw strength from it for years to come. I have good friends, a lovely home, an interesting job, and plenty of stimulating, creative spare time interests. What is most important, however, is that I have a balance in my life, and an inner wisdom that grows as I live and experience more. My childhood experiences have brought me lots of wisdom and strength. Even if everything else were taken from me, no one could take away my inner strength and wisdom – quite the contrary.

REFERENCES

Anthony, E James & Cohler, Bertram (Ed.) *The Invulnerable Child* Guilford Press, New York 1987

Beardslee, W., Podofresky, D. *Resilient Adolescents whose Parents Have Serious Affective and Other Psychiatric Disorders: The Importance of Self-understanding and Relationships.* American Journal of Psychiatry 145:63-69, 1988.

Claezon, Ingrid *Against all Odds: Children of Drug Abusers Speak about their Growing-up* (in Swedish) Mareld,Stockholm 1996

Dugan, Timothy & Coles, Roberts (Ed.) *The Child in Our Times: Studies in the Development of Resiliency* Brunner/Mazel, New York 1989

Erickson, Milton H & Rossi *Man: Evolving Consciousness and Identity in Hypnotherapy* Brunner/Mazel, New York 1989

Finkerhor, David & Berliner, Lucy *Research on the Treatment of Sexually Abused Children: A Review and Recommendations,* Journal of American Academy of Child and Adolescent Psychiatry, Vol 34 No 11, 1995

Freedman, Suzanne & Enright, Robert *Forgiveness as Goal with Incest Survivors,* Journal of Consulting and Clinical Psychology, Vol 64 No 5, 1996

Flanigan, Beverly *Forgiving the Unforgivable* Macmillan, New York 1994

Frankl, Viktor E *Man's Search for Meaning*

Goldstein, Howard *Victors or Victims: Contrasting Views of Clients in Social Work Practice.*

Hargrave,Terry *Families and Forgiveness: Healing Wounds in the Intergenerational Family* Brunner/Mazel, New York 1994

Hellsten, Tommy *The Hippopotamus in the Living Room.Co-dependency and the Encounter with the Inner Child* (In Finnish) Kirjapaja 1991.

Kaminer,Wendy *I'm Dysfunctional, You're Dysfunctional* Addison-Wesley, New York 1992

Kaufman, Joan & Zigler, Edward *Do Abused Children Become Abusive Parents?* American Journal of Orthopsychiatry 57, 1987

Loftus, Elisabeth F *Repressed Memory Accusations: Devastated families and Devastated Patients,* Applied Cognitive Psychology Vol 11, 1997

Moravia, Alberto & Elkann, Alain *Vita di Moravia* Bompiani, Milano 1990

Muller, Wayne *Legacy of the Heart: The Spiritual Advantages of a Painful Childhood* Simon & Schuster,New York 1992

Renaud, H & Estess, F. *Life History Interviews with 100 Normal American Males: "Pathogenicity" of Childhood.* American Journal of Orthopsychiatry 31,1961

Reviere, Susan *Memory of Childhood Trauma: A Clinician's Guide to Literature* Guilford Press, New York 1996

Roese, Neil & Olson, James *What Might Have Been: The Social Psychology of Counterfactual Thinking,* Lawrence Erlbaum Assoc., New Jersey 1995

Rutter, M & Quilton D *Long-term Follow-up of Women Institutionalized in Childhood Factors Promoting Good Functioning in Adult Life,* British Journal of Developmental Psychology Vol 2, 1984

Räsänen, Eila *Finnish Children of War: The effect of separation experiences during childhood on the mental and physical health and social well-being in adulthood : a psychosocial study of the later effects of war-child Separation.* Doctoral Dissertation in Finnish with an English Summary. Kuopio University Press, Kuopio 1998.

Saleebey, Dennis (Ed.) *The Strengths Perspective in Social Work Practice,* Longman, New York 1992

Seligman, Martin E *What You Can Change and What You Can't,* Alfred A Knopf, New York 1994

Simon, Richard *Behind the One-Way Kaleidoscope: The Strategic Therapy of Cloé Madanes Has a Logic of Its Own,*The Family Therapy Networker Sept 1986

Solantaus,Tytti & Beardslee, William *An Intervention to Prevent Psychological Disturbances in Children* (In Finnish)Duodecim 112,1996

Taylor, Shelley E *Positive Illusions: Creative Self-Deception and the Healthy Mind,* Basic Books,USA, 1989

Werner, Emmy & Smith, Ruth *Overcoming the Odds: High Risk Children from Birth to Adulthood* Cornell University Press, Ithaca, NY 1992.

Werner,Emmy & Smith, Ruth *Vulnerable but invincible* McGrawHill, N.York 1982

Wolin, Steve & Wolin, Sybil *The Resilient Self: How Survivors of Troubled Families Rise Above Adversity* Villard Books, New York 1993

Bibliography

Books and articles by Ben Furman

Solution Talk: Hosting Therapeutic Conversations. W.W. Norton & Co. New York, 1992. (co-authored with Tapani Ahola)

Pickpockets In A Nudist Camp: The Systemic Revolution In Psychotherapy. A collection of articles published elsewhere. Dulwich Centre Publications. Adelaide, South Australia, 1992.

Solution Talk: The Solution-Oriented Way of Talking about Problems. A chapter in: *Constructive Therapies*, Michael Hoyt (Ed.) Pages 41-66. Guilford Press, New York, 1994.

Criticism of Psychotherapy: Attack is the Best Form of Defence. A paper exploring the various psychological counter-manoeuvres utilised by representatives of the psychotherapeutic establishment to ward off any criticism against psychotherapy by directing it back onto the critic. Human Systems: The Journal of Systemic Consultation and Management, pages 47-56, Vol. 2. (1) 1991.

The Never Ending Story: The Problem as the Solution. A paper consisting of three linked cases describing the idea that problems can sometimes be viewed as solutions. Australian and New Zealand Journal of Family Therapy, 1991, Vol. 12, No 1; Pages 53-55.

Glasnost Therapy: Removing the Barriers between Client and Therapist. This paper discusses a new approach to teaching and consultation where clients, professionals and students are all invited to sit in the same room and communicate openly with each other about any ideas. The Family Therapy Networker May/June 1990, Pages 61-63 & 70.

The Chicken and the Egg: A Hindsight View of Therapy. This paper discusses the idea that what therapists think is the cause of problems is determined by what they intend to do to solve it rather than vice versa. Journal of Family Therapy 1989, Vol. 11, Pages 217-230.

Adverse Effects of Psychotherapeutic Beliefs. An appraisal of the potential negative effects of the most common etiologic assumptions of psychological problems. Journal of Systems Medicine 1989,7 (No 2), Pages 183-195.

Giving Consultation to one's Parents: What is a Task for? A case study describing the use of a strategic approach where the client is supervised to assist his parents to help him overcome his problems with excessive use of alcohol. Case Studies 1989, 3 (No 1), Pages 19-23.

The Return of the Question Why: The Advantages of Exploring Pre-Existing Explanations. Family Process 1988, 27 (No 4), Pages 395-409.

The Seven Illusions. A constructivist article describing seven different sources of the frequent clinical illusion that what we believe about our clients is in fact reality. The Family Therapy Networker 1988, Sept./Oct, Pages 30-31.

The Use of Humour in Brief Therapy. Published as an article in a special section on humour edited by Richard Belson and Ben Furman. Journal of Strategic and Systemic Therapies 1988, 7 (No 2), Pages 3-20.

About The Author

Dr. Ben Furman is a psychiatrist and internationally renowned authority on brief solution-oriented therapy. He teaches an approach to therapy where the emphasis is on resources rather than failings, on solutions rather than problems. Due to his infectious optimism, humour and creativity, Dr. Furman has been invited to teach at workshops and conferences around the world. In addition to teaching in Finland, where he is based, and the rest of Scandinavia, he has given workshops in the USA, Great Britain, Ireland, Germany, Austria, Spain, Italy, Hungary, Israel, Russia, Australia and New Zealand. His books and articles have been translated into many languages including English, German, Swedish, Danish, Spanish and Russian.

Nor is Dr. Furman's teaching restricted to professionals. In recent years he has started to teach his ideas to others interested in learning how to solve psychological and relational problems in a positive and empowering way. He has also been teaching staff at many companies, government agencies, schools and in other working environments. A frequent guest on Finnish television and radio programmes, he has been hosting his own TV talk-show where he discusses psychological problems and their solutions with his guests and live audience on Finnish National TV.

For more information about Dr. Furman you can visit his web pages at www.reteaming.com